TO: Grandpa &
Grandma a&b

From Evan

Merry christmas
Enjoy

(P.S) d'm on pag
240

OUR HONOURED HEROES

(FRONT COVER PHOTOS)

Martha Attema	Dean McCubbin	Christine Fortin	Doug McDonald	Lynn Johnston
Pages 98, 106 & 235	Page 50	Page 171	Page 115	Page 167

Bryan Sargent	Annie Percival	Lou Valenti	Jennifer Richmond Page 213 Jeremy Harkness Page 216	Shawn Venasse
Page 72	Page 131	239		Page 17

NORTH BAY - ONTARIO

INSPIRING STORIES BY AND ABOUT THE PEOPLE OF OUR REGION

Barry Spilchuk
Penny Tremblay
&
The Citizens of North Bay
and Surrounding Area

You're My Hero Books Ltd.
North Bay, ON

www.YMHbooks.com

Library of Congress Cataloging-in-Publication Data

You're My Hero™ - North Bay: Inspiring stories by and about the people
of our region/ Barry Spilchuk, Penny Tremblay and the Citizens
of North Bay, Ontario

ISBN 978-1-4276-2771-1 (trade paper)
1. Inspiration - I. Spilchuk, Barry; II. Tremblay, Penny; III. Title: You're My
Hero - North Bay

Publisher: You're My Hero Books Ltd.
               9 Carriage Crescent
               North Bay, ON Canada P1C 1G5

Executive Editor - Karen Spilchuk
Senior Editor - Carolyn Samuel
Cover design and layout by Laura Little
Cover photo by Greg McGuinty
Photo of Martha Attema by M.J. Hayes
Photo of Karen and Barry Spilchuk by Grace Boogers & Beryl Coakley

DEDICATION

*With love we dedicate this work to
all the citizens - past, present and future
of North Bay and surrounding area*

*We are proud of our region,
our history and the efforts of all the
people who have made this what we call . . .*
HOME

*We're going to be in a book
with a Chicken Soup guy!*

MAY WE MAKE A SUGGESTION?

If you have taken the time to share your Hero's name with us, you should find both of your names on the Honour Roll that starts on the next page.

If you are giving this book to your Hero, you may want to take a moment and say something like,

"We have known each other for awhile. I honour you as a friend (or family member) and I wanted you to know - you are one of my heroes too."

If you are the Hero who has been named in this book, take a second and think about what has just happened.

Someone took the time to think about who their hero is. They even took the time to share it with us.

And they picked...You!

You're my **Hero**™

Authors and Heroes

HONOUR ROLL

Location: if a **number** *is shown, the story can be found on that specific page in this book. If the letters* **WS** *are shown, the story can be seen on our website:* ***www.YMHbooks.com*** *(click on MAP of current projects). If a "-" is shown, the author simply wanted to list their name and their hero's name. There is no story.*

Writer's Name	Hero's Name	Location
Adams, Alexander	Wayne Poeta	-
Adams, Samantha	Wayne Poeta	-
Adams, Sherri	Kim Adams	-
Adams, Sue	Wayne Poeta	-
Ahmed, Iman	God	-
Allen, Brandon	Bert Allen	WS
Allen, Scott	Robert Allen	WS
Allison, Tayler	Joelle Allison	WS
Allison, Tayler	Amy Hurtubise	24
Alkins, Karly	Dora Alkins	WS
Amos, Anastasia	Stacy Lynn Melrose	242
Amyotte, Brad	Norm Gauthier	WS
Anderson, Michelle	Margaret Anderson	WS
Andrews, Connor	Mark Andrews	WS
Aniol, Angela	Christopher Aniol	WS
Anthony, Des	Michael Bubnich	218
Arseneault, Mathew	Elucippe Arseneault	WS
Ashley, Debbie	John Ashley	WS
Aultman, Deb	Joe Aultman	WS
Aultman, Nancy	Laurie, Jason, Vanessa Shaelyn, Kadin Laronde	WS

Writer's Name	Hero's Name	Location
Austin, Mike	Barry Austin	61
Avery, Jessica	Karen Guilfoyle	-
Bahm, Matt	Canada's Unknown Soldier	180
Ballentine, Holly Elizabeth	Heather Ballentine	226
Baran, Keltan	Ralf the Hamster	WS
Baril, Brandon	Colby Ricker	123
Barton, Paul	Glenna Barton	WS
Barton, Sarah	Paul Barton	-
Bastien, Laurel	Diane Twomey	WS
Beadle, Kara	Dr. Renee Porter	128
Beadle, Kara	Dr. Paul Thistle	WS
Beardmore, Denise	Brad Beardmore	WS
Beaudoin, Craig	Elton Paynter	WS
Beauparlant-Turpin, Diane	Carmen Turcot	WS
Belanger, Amanda	Marie Belanger	WS
Belanger, Graham	Cathy Belanger	-
Belanger, Jessica	Patty McCulloch	WS
Belanger, Jilllian	Cathy Belanger	-
Bernardi, Sarah	Lynne Bernardi	WS
Betts, Nancy	Dr. Michael Allen	-
Binewych-Helliwell, Zenon	Pamela Binewych-Helliwell	WS
Biffis-Kri, Sandy	Dick Wyga	57
Blumsom, Bradley	John Blumsom	WS
Bodley, Joseph	Steven	WS
Boissonneault, Samantha-Ann	Leo Jobin	WS
Boissonneault, Samantha-Ann	Argentina Pigeau	133
B., Dane	Peter Bolton	WS
Bond, Mitchell	Sherry Semeniuk	228
Bowes, Mike	Brian Bowes	242
Brideau, Michael	Brideau, Mike	WS
Brogan, Kendell	Robert Brogan	WS
Bros, Erin	Zak Mullin	26
Brooks, Helen	Gilles Berube	WS
Brooks, Kiersten	Liz Brooks	47
Brown, Chelsey	Diane Johanson	188

Writer's Name	Hero's Name	Location
Brown, Sharon	Shannon Desrosiers	WS
Brown, Talia	Herb Brown	**156**
Brown, Tammy	Lynn Bull	WS
Bucknell, Nicole	Colette Landry	**198**
Bullock, Lexie	Helga Paas	WS
Burke, Brianna	My Family & Jesus	-
Burke, Zacc	My Family	-
Burton, Ryan	Dion Phaneuf	**173**
Caley, Marley Anne	Chantalle Battiston	**262**
Caine, Jon	David Caine	WS
Calder, Sommer Christi	Mira deBois	WS
Caliciuri, Melissa	Gerhild Hildebrand (Oma)	-
Caliciuri, Sabina	Gerhild Hildebrand (Oma)	-
Caliciuri-Hildebrand Susan	Gerhild Hildebrand	-
Cameron, Jesse	Moofa	**110**
Cameron, Sophie	Moofa	WS
Carneiro-Bowman Kristena	Carolyn Samuel	**185**
Carr, Jesse	Bud Alcorn & Matthew Carr	-
Carr, Patricia	Chriss Wagner	**258**
Carew, Maire	My Husband	-
Cauvier, Sherry	Marie Morin	-
Celentano, Ralph	Francis Celentano	-
Chadbourn, Chelsea	Grandma Lynda & Madeleine	WS
Churchman, Daisy	Lorraine Nevill	-
Chute, Laura	Kathy Chute	WS
Citizens of North Bay	Bob McIntyre	-
Citizens of North Bay	Chris Thacker	-
Citizens of North Bay	Hank the Paper Boy	-
Claridge, Jessica	David Whitesell	WS
Clark, Cheryl	Scott Clark	-
Clark, Mandy	Jennifer Lyn Richmond	WS
Clark, Matthew	Barry Berger	WS
Clark, Scott	Cheryl Clark	-
Clarke, Kelly	Capt. Paul Clarke	WS
Clarke, Peggy	Staff at C.H.E.O.	WS

Writer's Name	Hero's Name	Location
Clarke, Peggy	Aunt Tootsie	WS
Clarke, Peggy	Kim Clarke	WS
Clarkes, Art & Lucy	Chris M. Samson	WS
Clifford, Dawson	Andreena Clifford	-
Close, Matthew	Daniel Close	WS
Clouthier, Trista	Elwood Piché	WS
Cole, Cameron	John Marcil	243
Collins, Amanda	James Collins	WS
Collins, Carley	Dennis Molloy	147
Congiano, Holly	Kevin Oschefski	-
Conlon, Courtney	Rosemary Conlon	WS
Cook, Abby	Shawn Venasse	17
Cook, Victoria	Danielle Trudeau	260
Cook, Victoria	Paige Shemilt	260
Cooper, Luke	Maria Cooper	-
Couroux, Brianna	Cathy Morris	-
Cowan, Chris	Ian Cowan	116
Cowan, Samantha	Chris Cowan	212
Culin, Matthew	Fred Culin	243
Cundari, Glenn	Joe Cundari	-
Dagg, Daryl	Lucille Beauvais	WS
Dahl, Jessica	Jacob Raymond Prediger	151
Dampier, Craig	Robert Dampier	63
Daniel, Maggie	Amanda Pollard	WS
Daniel, Maggie	Jerri Clout	12
Daniels, Lauren	Laurie Daniels	243
Daniher, Jen	Her Friends	WS
Danis, Ginette	Donald Danis	WS
Danis, Ginette	Roch Danis	WS
Daly, Susan	Kayla Carapanta	-
Davis, Bethany	John Davis	-
Davis, Tracy	Greg Brewer	-
Demaine, Shirley	Charlotte Smith	28
Denis, Bryan	Alain Denis	-
Denis, Steven Guy	Al Denis	WS

Writer's Name	Hero's Name	Location
Desilets, Dana	Debra Desilets	-
Desrosiers, Rolly & Michelle	Bryce Desrosiers	WS
Deveau, Kurt	The Homeless	WS
Deveau, Mirand May	Clint Pourde	WS
Deveau, Sharita-May	Clint Pourde	WS
Devine, Katelyn	Pattie Olson	WS
Dhami, Sophie	Ann Guilfoyle	WS
Dibb, Judy LaBrash	Audrey Irene (MacDonald) Labrash	WS
Dimmel, Josh	Billy Talent	-
Dobson, Cassie	Ylise Dobson	WS
Donovan-McDonald, Judy	Bernie Donovan	**76**
Doody, Alexandria	Crystal Doody	-
Dorval, Megan	Colleen Dorval	WS
Dorval, Stacey	Colleen Dorval	WS
Dorval, Stacey	Anonymous Doctor	WS
Doucet, Steven	Paula Doucet	-
Doucette-Minor, Linda	Chantal Michaud, Priscilla Barnes	WS
Doucette-Minor, Linda	Rose Brule Doucette	WS
Drenth, Cameron	Dave Drenth	-
Drenth, Emily	Martha Attema	**98**
Drenth, Kayleigh	Barb Drenth	**45**
Dufort, Carson	Laura Hann	-
Duhaime, Jason	Lynda Marshall	WS
Duncan, Rhonda	Helen Duncan	**41**
Dushnitskaya, Luba	Amy DeGenova	**6**
Eastman, Todd	Lance Armstrong	-
Elliott, Charles	Marilyn Elliott	-
Elliott, Drew	Heather Elliott	WS
Emmerson, Meagan	Emily Gough	WS
Emond-Galan, Kierra	Tracie Galan	**42**
Emond-Galan, Kierra	Mac Emond	WS
Erven, Craig	Chuck Erven	WS
Farella, Ben	Jacob Bentley Farella, Roman and Matteo Farella	-

Writer's Name	Hero's Name	Location
Farquhar, Katelyn	Tracy Farquhar	WS
Feltz, Teagan	Duane Feltz	-
Feltz, Travis	Rosey & Orville Feltz	98
Fennell, Jody	Harold Fennell	244
Fetterly, Kyle	Matt Kenseth	-
Fitzgerald, Amanda	Martin Conville	WS
Fleguel, Bailey	Kirk Fleguel	-
Fleury, Stephen	Ronald McIntyre	144
Foren, Danielle	Benjamin Tafe	WS
Forsyth, Samantha	Gerry Forsyth	WS
Forth, Katie	Emily Gough	19
Forth-Samson, Belinda	Stewart Robertson	WS
F., K.	Diana	WS
Frame, Jeffrey	My Mom	WS
Fraser, Ally Claire Joan	Joan Fraser	130
Fraser, Madison	Grandma Hugs	WS
Freeson, Madison	Leslie Vanderburg	35
Freeston, Jamie-Lee	Hannah Latour	WS
Fudger, Kristina	Dianne Fudger	-
Fung, Rachel	Nicholas Fung	219
Gagne, Rebecca-Ann	Dawn Antonissen	190
Gagne, Sharon	Derek Gagne	WS
Gagné, Vince	Ronald Gagné	-
Gallagher, John	Bruce Middlestead	-
Gammon, Sarah	Guy & Julie Gammon	WS
Garcia, Chantal	Natalie Garcia	WS
Gilligan, Valerie	Carey Gilligan	WS
Giroux, Rita	Donna Nielsen, Karen Giroux-Byers	WS
Goldfarb, Eli	Abraham Goldfarb	230
Goldfarb, Jacob	Sandra Bloomberg	232
Goldfarb, Rose	Bubby Rose Goldfarb	99
Goodridge, Lindsay	Alice Graham	-
Goodridge, Lindsay	Sarah Loretto	-
Goodyear, Scott	James Godfrey Goodyear	WS

Writer's Name	Hero's Name	Location
Hill, Tiffany	Morris Fricker	WS
H., D.	Ingrid Himmelman	WS
Hirsh, Allan	Lynn Johnston	-
Hives, Emma	Lucky – My Cat	WS
Hoffman, Kevin	David Gilmore	-
Holden, Catherine	Jack Jones	-
Holden, Catherine	Reberta Bedard	-
Hoover, Hayley	My Dad - Raymond	WS
Hopkins, Andrew	Audna Savage	WS
Howard, Caitlin	Mary Flemming	138
Houle, Anthony	Joey Van Stroe	WS
Hughes, Cheryl	Jess Larochelle	112
Hughes, Morgan	My Dog Tess	WS
Humphrey-Cusmanic, Shannon	Gerald Humphrey	59
Hunt, Alexandria-Alicia	Silvano Urbano	WS
Hunt, Dan	Peter McKeown	-
Hurst, Jessica	George Hurst	WS
Hurst, Jessica	Kathy Hurst	WS
Ibbitson, Josh	Family	WS
Inthof, Brittany	Christina Hinds	30
Irwin, Hannah	Dr. Karen Morris	100
Irwin, Sarah	Jody Stockfish	101
J., Chelsea	Mrs. Mary J	WS
Jackson, Regan	Bryon Jackson	WS
Jamieson, Brett	Anna Wintar	WS
Jenkins, Lorna	Alma Mallette	-
Jessup, Sheila	Jim Jessup	-
Jewell, Amanda	Heather Jewell	WS
Jewell, Amanda	Lucky the Deer	252
Jewell, Ashley	Brenda Mansell	WS
Jewell, Ashley	Rosita Brassard	WS
Jodouin, Dakota	Peggy Clarke	126
Jodouin, Sarah-Jane	Brittany Scappatura	WS
Johnson, Mary Ann	Joyce Johnson	-
Johnston, Ashley	Fay Johnston	WS

Writer's Name	Hero's Name	Location
Jordan, Brent	Jim Jordan	**101**
Jordan, Jeffry	Jim Jordan	-
Kaminski-Morneault, Sonia	Cliff Noth	**266**
K., B.	Aidan Shipley	WS
Keech, Beth	Michele & William Keech	WS
Kellar, Stacy	Bill Gates	-
Kent, Brandy	Pam Kent	WS
Kidson, Sally	Mark Gilligan	**223**
King, Jocelyn	Alexandra King	-
King, Jodie	Mike Wright	**191**
King, Mark	Don King	-
Kitchen, Abeba	Tracy Kennedy	**21**
Kraft, Amanda	Yaeko Kraft	WS
Kuehni, Jenny	Walter Walker	**142**
Knox, John	Lou Valenti	**239**
L.R.B., Aurora	Mark Caldwell	WS
Ladouceur, Cam	Rob Ladoucer	-
Lafantaisie, Stephanie	Jay MacDonald	WS
Lafontaine, Suzanne	Elucippe Arseneault	WS
Lafreniere, Janine	Jeannine Coutu	-
Lamont, Katlyn	Emily Guzzo	-
Lamont, Katlyn	Steph Lamont	-
Lanctot, Nicholas	Larry Lanctot	WS
Landry, Donny	Lisa Landry	WS
Laferriere, Jessie	Tammy Laferriere	-
Laperriere, Cassandra	Cathy Laperrriere	**39**
L., Tina	Alexandria Dawn	WS
Lavoie, Lynn	Claudette Lafontaine	-
L., C	Matt	-
Leblanc, Ashley	Nathalie Leblanc	**36**
LeBlanc, Molly McKenzie	Brenda LeBlanc	**135**
Lecappelain, Serena	Melissa Chapin	WS
Lechlitner, Evan	Andrew Bubarh	**240**
Ledoux, Ryan	Michelle Trudeau	WS
Ledoux, Ryan	Sean Ledoux	WS

Writer's Name	Hero's Name	Location
Lefebvre, Jerry	Pat Lefebvre	-
Lefebvre, Michel	Connie & Rene Lefebvre	-
Lefebvre, Pat	Edith Love	-
Lemay, Mario	Suzanne Harmony	-
Lemay, Mario	Sharon Rivet	-
Lennips, Jamie	Sgt. Jim Lennips	244
Lennips, Julia	Jim Lennips	-
Levesque, Jackie	Lynn Johnston	167
Levesque, Josie	Betty Hurley	WS
Liamzina, Liuba	Lynn Johnston	167
Liberty, Kayla	Kathy Moring	WS
Liesmer-Turco, Kelly	Family	WS
Little, Heather	Marvin Little	-
Little, Laura	James and Laura Sneddon	-
Little, Mary-Rose	Rosalie Little	132
Lobb, Jeff	Grace St. George	WS
Lockhart, Jack	Alexander Davidson	153
Loponen, Shelley	Kathy Sirrs	83
Love, Courtney	Cathy & Grant Love	WS
Loveridge, Nicole	Kathy Loveridge	-
Loveridge, Sarah	Kathy Loveridge	WS
Luesby-Gravelle, Cindy	Special Students	201
MacAulay, Kristy	Angie MacAulay	WS
MacLellan, Jillian	Kathryn MacLellan	245
MacNeill, Alyssa	Michele MacNeill	WS
Mah, Kate	Martha Attema	-
Major, Alice	Rachel E. Knight	WS
Major, Cheryl	Homer Joseph Major	WS
Malden, Gail	Daryl Malden	-
Manning, Jenna	Karen Manning	-
Manning, Sara	Karen Manning	102
Marshall, Lynda	Barb Weeks	8
Marshall, Steve	Walter Marshall	108
Marson, Debbie	Heath Marson	-
Marson, Debbie	Alice Radley	-

Writer's Name	Hero's Name	Location
Marson, Heath	Debbie Marson	-
Maslova, Alexandra	Mikhail Chaikin	WS
Mason, Lucas	Brenda Brooks	WS
Mason, Solomon	Brenda Brooks	44
Mason, Tyler	Heather Priolo	136
Masse, Kim	Sally Scott	-
Mastellar, Margie	The Quiet Cowboy	174
Mathias, Brooke	Demi Lynn Mathias	-
Matte, Kira	Deborah Matte	-
McArthur, Judith	George McArthur & Jack Weller	-
McCann, Kaitlin	Kathie Chapman	WS
McCann, Megan	Albina McCann	WS
McLellan, Evelyn	Lorraine Knuth	WS
McCrea, Dana	Lori-Ann Coffin	264
McCubbin, Rob	Dean McCubbin	50
McDonald, Kaitlyn	Al & Doreen Hodgins	WS
McIsaac, Peggy	Bill Peacock	182
McMillan, Lloyd	Jesus Christ	164
McNeill, Alyssa	Michele McNeill	WS
McQuoid, Brady	Mitchell McQuoid	-
McQuoid, Kelly	Dave McQuoid	-
McRae, Gen	Don McRae	-
Meechan, Jody	Alexiss Meecham	WS
Meldrum, Jacob	Jessie Johnson	246
Menard, Athena	Athena Menard	-
Michaud, Annie	Nathalie Ouellet	-
Miller, Kenzie	Jody Shaddick	WS
Minor, Camille	Chantal Michaud	-
Mishquart, Kasey	Simon Mishquart	WS
Mishquart, Kasey	Albert Starka	118
Mitchell, Amanda	Erin Robertson	196
Montgomery, Jeremy	Michael Larochelle	WS
Morawski, M.	L. Morawski	WS
Moore, Robert W.	Phyllis Bell	255
Moore, Rod	Linda Beatty	268

Writer's Name	Hero's Name	Location
Mortson, Vern	Doug McDonald	115
Mulligan, James	James Frederick Mulligan	WS
Neff, Nicole	Paul Neff	-
Neil, David	Penny Tremblay	-
Neil, Ryan	Jeff Gordon #24	-
Neil, Ryan	Dave Neil	-
Neil, Sierra	Dave Neil	-
Nevrencan, Maiya	Mom, Brother, Aunt, Martha Attema	102
Newton, Janna	Albert Graham Coulter	-
Nicholas, Erika	Mary Purcell	WS
Nicholson, Joy Marie	All my friends	WS
Nodwell, Jane Sargent	Brenda Fetterly	WS
Noth, Hutton	Gerry "Nono" Nori	-
O'Connell, Jamie	Lucy Ricci	-
O'Donnell, Frances	Patricia Ellen Dawson	WS
Olivier, David	Lynne Roy	257
Ortiz, Triana	Jane Ortiz	WS
Osburn, John	Elizabeth Rothery	Wall
Osmond, Joanne	Eileen Osmond	WS
Osmond, Joanne	Ralph Downey	WS
Ouellette, Andre	Tammy Corbeil	WS
Ovens, Sam	Hero in Everyone	WS
Page, Beth	Carl Page	WS
Page, Lauren	Jake the Dog	WS
Page, Lauren	My Mom	WS
P., Diane	Melissa	WS
Patterson, Cora	David Byers	124
Paul, Jayne	"JAPS"	WS
P., Clara	Neal	WS
Pecore, Rory	Dan	WS
Pecore, Zach	Steve Omischl	179
Peer-Ranger, Kelly	Lois Peer	-
Penney, Bernard	Linda Penney	-
Perrault, Cathy	Rick Legault	-

Writer's Name	Hero's Name	Location
Perron, Noah	Eileen Larmer	245
Petrant-Rennie, Nicole	Aqua & Birk Rennie	WS
Petten, V.	Erica Bainbridge	WS
Phillips, Mark	Kristy Armstrong	WS
Piché, Elizabeth	My Brother	WS
Piché, Laura	Lynn Johnston	167
Pitman, Jessica	Holly Brisebois	-
Point, Marshall	God	103
Power, Michael-Anthony	Enzo & Rose Valenti	WS
Preston, Jayla	Tom Preston	WS
Preston, Teagan	Shelley Preston	WS
Preston, Tessa	Jare	WS
PJ, Frank	Everyone	WS
Purtell, Laurie	Barb Driver	WS
Racine, Mary Jo	Michel Racine	-
Rancourt, Kayla	Krista Newhook	WS
Ratra, Varun Atul	Sumita Ratra	WS
Raycraft, Lyndsay	Gordon Ashford	-
Razaly, Zainab	Syeda Gilani	103
Reid, Debbie	Sam Hodgson	64
Reid, Deborah	Greg Birtch	WS
Reischer, Josh	My Mystery Girl	WS
Rhoads, Tanner	Matt Darnell	-
Richardson, Brennan	Cameron Buckle	104
Richardson, Peggy	Tyler Richardson	WS
Richmond, Ann	Jennifer Richmond	213
Richmond, Jennifer	Jeremy Harkness	-
Rick, Amanda	Jo-ann Rick	-
Ricketts, Danielle	Peter Ricketts	53
Riley, Kendra Emily Sarah	Cindy Riley	WS
Rioux, Helen	Claude Rioux	WS
Rocheleau, Diane	Brian, Adam, and Samantha Rocheleau	WS
Robidoux, Meghan	Christine Fortin	171
Robillard, Elizabeth	Eli Robillard	-

Writer's Name	Hero's Name	Location
Robinson, Ashley	Molly Penny	251
Robinson, Stephanie	Ashley Robinson	WS
Rodgers, Dave	Susan Rodgers	-
Rogerson, Sue	Pastor Daniel Bjorkman	-
Rootes, Ryan	Joel Johnson	WS
Rowley, Brent	Ed Rowley	-
Roy, Brittany	Regis Young	159
Ryan, Hana	Hannah Irwin	104
Ryan, Victoria	Deborah Ryan	-
Ryan, Victoria	Michael Ryan	-
Samantha	Meghan	-
Samuel, Carolyn	Scott & Cheryl Clark	14
Samuel, Carolyn	Greg & Gail Samuel	204
Samuel, Gail	Milton Wallace Smith	88
Santos, Gilbert	Emanuel Santos	-
Sapinski, Tom	George Edgerton	146
Sargent, Katie	Bryan Sargent	72
Savage, Kristen	Keith & Erik Savage	WS
Savard, Lynn Ellen	Florence (Flo) Jones	WS
Savoie, Josee	Priscille Savoie	WS
Scanlan, Colleen	Annie Percival	131
Schamerhorn, Sarah	James Herriot	WS
Schroter, Carolyn	Roberta Schroter	WS
Scott, Jake	Tom Scott	-
Sebalj, Kayla	Hayley Sebalj	207
Seguin, Angèle	Joel	WS
S., Damian	Darren Jackson	-
Serson, Amanda	Mike Croghan	WS
Serson, Amanda	Jordan Gardiner	WS
Servello, Kassandra	Carmen Servello	WS
Sharma, Chetna	Mahadev Sharma	-
Shultz, Kim	Nichola K.S Goddard	WS
Siepmann, Judy	Gwen Maguire-Loverock	WS
Sirrs, Katelyn	Kathryn Sirrs	32
Sloan, Tracy	Melvina Novack	139

Writer's Name	Hero's Name	Location
Smit, Irene	Alan Dayes	-
Smith, Kaitlin	Susan Smith	WS
Smith, Lynda	Barbara Saunders	**80**
Smith, Monique	Marc Smith	-
Snyder, Katelyn	My Parents	-
Sohm, Gail M.	Mary, a Worshiper	WS
Soucie, Charlene	Dr. Steven	WS
Soucie, Charlene	My family	WS
Spiess, Mackenzy	Kcristal Spiess	WS
Spilchuk, Allie	Shirley Duchesne	**92**
Spilchuk, Barry	Karen Spilchuk	-
Spilchuk, Billy	Edward Toner	**149**
Spilchuk, Christine	Karen Spilchuk	-
Spilchuk, Eugene	Bill Semkiw	-
Spilchuk, Jamie	Cat McCormick	-
Spilchuk, Joyce	Barry Spilchuk	-
Spilchuk, Karen	Gil Gove	-
Spilchuk, Karen	Margaret Gove	-
Spilchuk, Mike	Eugene Spilchuk	**162**
Spilchuk, Tim	Joe Soron	-
Spykerman, Meaghan	Terry Fox	WS
Stanley, Chantal	Wisgona the Horse	WS
St. Onge, Matt	Doug Hermeston	**113**
St. Onge, Matt	The Unnoticed Heroes	**2**
Steel, Mark	Samantha Steel	-
Steel, Peter	Jesus	WS
Stephens, Jessica	Brian Stephens	**68**
Stephenson, Shaye	Dr. Steven Steinberg	105
Stevens, Alyssa	Vivian	WS
Stevens, Jennifer	Aaron Beaucage	WS
Stevenson, Tracy	Alex Stevenson	-
Stewart, Emily	Gaetane Stewart	WS
Stewart, Emily	Gordon Stewart	WS
Stewart, Jennifer	Sandra Stewart	105
Stuart, Adam Lorne	Jesus Christ	WS

Writer's Name	Hero's Name	Location
Sullivan, James	Eddie Vedder	177
Sullivan, Sherry	Abe & Olive Joseph	119
Sullivan, Tanner	Shana Sullivan	-
Sutherland, Trina Marie	Monique Sutherland	WS
Sykes, Megan	Gary McLeod	-
Swain, Noah	Mrs. Swell Standan	WS
Taylor, Kay-Sea	Maria Muto	WS
Taylor, Lauren	Doug Taylor	WS
TenEyck, Kenzie	Noella TenEyck	WS
Thesen, Philip	Sonja Thesen	WS
Thomas, Ian	Debbie Thomas	WS
Thomas, Sydney	Trevor Thomas	106
Tranter, Madison	Theresa Moran	245
Tucker, Denicia	Uncle Gary Seniuk	WS
Torpy, Moreen	Orleana Fraser	-
Tougas, Larry	George Tougas	95
Tremblay, Coretta	People of North Bay	WS
Tremblay, Penny	Ava Vosu	248
Truchon, Irene	Felix Truchon	-
Trudeau, Michelle	Mark Trudeau	-
Turco (Liesmer), Kelly	Rosemary, Terry, Mary Kay, Leo & Liz	WS
Turcotte, Carly	Glenn Turcotte	WS
Turcotte, Kelly Ann	Claire Turcotte	WS
Turcotte, Kessie	Mike St. Pierre	WS
Turcotte, Kessie	Jennnifer Deschamps	WS
Turgeon, Lisa Anne Marie	Vic & Monique Turgeon	WS
Turner, Natalie	Florence Trottier	-
Twilt, Shelby	Martin Luther King	WS
Udeschini, Lauren	Marc Udeschini	WS
Vaananen, Graeme	Marcie Gervais	184
Valade, Trisha Marie	Patricia Anne Duncan	WS
Valenti, Giulia	Marta Attema	106
Van Mierlo, Kim	Jacky Belford	-
Van Mierlo, Travis	Joseph Doxsee	WS

Writer's Name	Hero's Name	Location
Vander Valk, Jacky	Rob Vander Valk	71
Vander Valk, Rob	Jacky Vander Valk	70
VanDoleweerd, Stephanie	Lynn Johnston	167
Vendetti, Denise	Roseanne Lafleur	-
Vesterback, Cassandra	My Cat Tiger	WS
Viancourt, Daryl	Gilbert Viancourt	-
Vibe, Kayla	Marilyn Vibe	WS
Villeneuve, Jeannine	Nicole	WS
Virgin, Chris	Karen Virgin	WS
Walker, Lisa	Nancy Armstrong	46
Waller, Madison	My Dog Sheena	222
Ward, Tiffany	North Bay	-
Warren, Gloria	Bob Warren	WS
Watson, Jim	William "Bill" Oliver	90
Weegar, Jessica	Kristie Pinard	-
Welton, Jo-Anne	Sarah Welton	209
Werner, Mikayla	Mikayla Werner	270
Weyh, Rodney	My Parents	-
Whelan, Frances Ann	Peter Michael Whelan	WS
White, Bethan	Norman White	154
Whitney, April	Trista Clouthier	WS
Wilson, Kaitlyn	Ellen Wilson	WS
Willis, Mackenzie	Donald E. Willis	246
Witiuk, Lindsay	Rob Witiuk	65
Witmer, Chris	Ron Witmer	-
Wolfe, Dr. Bryan	George Wolfe	-
Wolfe, Chad	Victor Pasowisty	-
Wolfe, Chad	Judy Waymouth	-
Wood, Marlene	Eleanor McCarthy	WS
Wright, Jeanie	Christine Fortin	WS
Youmans, Sarah	Kristian Youmans	122
Ypya, Laurie	Elmer Ypya	-
Zadorozny, Allison	Lynn Johnston	167
Zamperoni, Kristen	Carolyn Keene	241
Zucchiatti, Peter	Lori Beckerton	-

SPECIAL HONOUR ROLL
Ms. Chan Crocker's Business Students
W.J. Fricker Senior Public School

8-F	8-G
Jessica Bartol	Aarin
Keenan B.	Greg
James Berti	Robert
Chris B.	Jordan
Brandon Burke	Laura
Alyssa Corbett	Alex
Justin Davis	Aaron
Jalyssa Davison	Philip
Kayleigh Drenth	Katie
Candice Gagnon	Brad
Brittney Glass	Bronson
Daniel Goulard	Davison
Ashley Greer	Becky
Turner Hampel	Cameron
Adam Hewitt	Kosh
Patrick Markert	Skye
Blake Martel	Greg
Allie O'Brien	Brian
Lauren Page	Alyssa
Terrence P.	Dawna
Mark Schoen	Kim
Jake Scott	Brittany
Damian S.	Saraya
Brittany Topham	Carly
Lisa Walker	Thomas
Brodey	

Mrs. Michelle Kangur - Educational Assistant

Greetings from
Vic Fedeli
Mayor, North Bay

A hero is defined as a person who wins recognition by noble deeds. In my capacity as Mayor of the City of North Bay, I see real heroes everyday.

Most heroes are people whose noble deeds go unheralded, but certainly not unnoticed. They are the folks who give of themselves for the benefit of others.

They are the people who volunteer their time to help out at a seniors' home, or coach a little league team. They are the people who raise money to fight disease, or help a struggling family. They are the people who really look around themselves and identify the needs of other people, and then do what they can to help. They are the people who take a moment to brighten someone else's day.

These are the unsung heroes that make such a vital difference in the lives of everyone in our city. On behalf of the citizens of North Bay, I want to thank Barry, Penny and all the contributors for shedding a little bit of light on these unheralded noble deeds and reminding us all who the real heroes in life truly are.

Victor Fedeli

Greetings from
Anthony Rota
M.P. Nipissing-Timiskaming

When I think of heroes, I think of ordinary people who perform extraordinary actions. A child who stands up for justice when a bully tries to push another child around in the schoolyard, a stranger who runs into a burning house to save a crying child, a soldier who puts his life on the line to protect his country, or a parent who teaches his or her child to make the world a better place.

Life presents us with challenges on a daily basis; how we react to those challenges is what makes us heroes or allows us to pass on the opportunity. When it comes down to it, a hero is determined by the actions taken when confronted with everyday challenges, large or small.

One thing is certain, the world is a better place because of the actions of heroes.

I commend Barry and Penny for putting this book together, allowing us to share our thoughts on our personal heroes, who they are and what actions they have taken to make North Bay, Canada and our world a better place.

Sincerely,

Anthony Rota

Greetings from
Monique Smith
M.P.P. Nipissing

Just what makes someone a hero? Over the span of a lifetime, the idea of a hero is bound to evolve. For a young child, a hero may be someone who scares away the monsters under your bed. Later in life, a hero might be a mom or dad, a teacher, a hockey coach, a youth group leader, or a police officer. Ultimately heroism is about giving of yourself for other people and the world around us.

I have had many heroes in my life; my mom and dad, who have shown such grace, love and compassion during difficult times in their lives while never veering from their commitment to their family and their community; people I have known who have faced serious medical issues and fought their battles with incredible courage and dignity; and, local volunteers who through their commitment to their local causes have improved the lives of many and our community as a whole.

Heroes like the ones highlighted in this book are vital to the make up of our community and are one of the biggest reasons that North Bay is such a great place to live. As Canadians, we often suffer from a modesty that makes us reluctant to celebrate those around us as heroes. There are so many individuals in our communities whose generosity is truly heroic. I am thrilled that this book will allow some to be recognized and celebrated.

I would like to thank Barry Spilchuk, Penny Tremblay and all those who submitted stories for making this book possible and allowing us to celebrate North Bay as the great place it is and its citizens as the heroes they are.

Monique Smith

Greetings from
Patricia Carr
North Bay & District Chamber of Commerce

I am excited by what this first book has done for our community, having school children show such enthusiasm about a project. Many others have also written in honour of their true heroes.

In most of the cases, the heroes are citizens from our city. I too submitted a story about my hero, which wasn't an easy task since I have quite a few heroes that have helped shape my life in a positive way.

Barry is a true champion in our community and he encourages businesses, community leaders as well as the citizens and children of our community to be their best.

What a great way to recognize all the people in our region and a special thanks to those that took the time to write their stories and show pride in North Bay and area - a great place to live and work.

Sincerely,

Patricia Carr

ACKNOWLEDGEMENTS

By co-author - Barry Spilchuk

To everyone who wrote a story and took the time to mail it, fax it, deliver it or submit it on-line - our eternal thanks!

Since this book is entirely about acknowledgement, we could go on and on about every name that is listed. Each of these people has contributed in some way to the overwhelming success of our concept.

To save a few trees, we have decided to list their names only. In a few cases, we just "have to" expand a little bit.

At this point in the book, our greatest fear is that we overlook or miss someone. If we miss or forget anyone – please accept our sincerest apologies and know that you and your contributions are appreciated.

From W. J. Fricker Senior Public School: Chan Crocker, Michelle Kangur and Donna Breault were the fuel that helped get this project into the hands of our current and future heroes - our children. Chan and Michelle dedicated many hours of their own time, and classroom time, as we used this book as a business-model for their grade-eight classes.We want to thank all of the W.J. Fricker students who enthusiastically embraced this project. We would also like to thank Mike Callahan, Sarah Spence, and the entire faculty and staff who gave us tremendous support.

From West Ferris Secondary School: Karen Bond is a super-hero, not only to her students and fellow faculty members; she is a hero for this book. With a thirty-second explanation of what this project was, she caught the "hero bug" and spread it throughout her school. Karen, you are a blessing! Principal Tim Collins caught the hero bug from Karen and welcomed us with open arms to share this concept with his entire school. Thanks to Dave McKenney and the entire faculty who helped on "You`re My Hero Day" and special thanks to teacher Larry Tougas who has the distinction of being the first person to submit a story for this book.

From Vincent Massey Public School: Martha Attema, Penny Lecour, Amanda Meighan, Marcie Gervais, Laurie Mantha, Alice Hennigar, Chris Francom, Jim Burrows, and staff.

From Chippewa Secondary School: Vince Gagné and John Humble, who opened their doors to let us in to do two assemblies so we could share with the students how they could participate in this project. Siobhan and Randy Mulroy, Michelle Graham, Nancy Dewar-Stenning, Andy Gagné, Carolyn Samuel (more about Carolyn later), and all the students who wrote stories and did posters and pre-sales - thank you so much!

From Widdifield Secondary School: Kelly Brown embraced this project almost one year before it was officially launched. Kelly's enthusiasm for this project went a long way towards us making our decision to press, "Go" and say, "Yes" to this amazing dream. Lynda Marshall, Rob McCubbin, and all the students, faculty, and staff, you are loved and appreciated more than we can say.

To all the children, staff, teachers and administration of the Near North School Board and the Nipissing-Parry Sound Catholic District School Board for opening the doors of possibility to our students – thank you.

From our city at large: thank you to - Frank O'Hagan, Dave Cerisano, Brent Labrosse, Laura Piché, Allison Zadorozny, Mike and Lori Venasse, Ed Regan, Christian Fortin, Marisa Knox, Katie Sargent, Colleen Scanlan, Julie Wright-McDonald, Ann Richmond and Tracy Vigars for their help in collecting photos of our front-cover honourees.

To our internal support team: Mike Spilchuk, Christine Spilchuk, Jamie Spilchuk, Joyce Spilchuk, Eugene Spilchuk, Gail Samuel, David and Marcia Treat, Kenny Markanich, and Brad Currie - each one of you has made a contribution to this book that has helped us move the whole project to a new level. God has blessed us with all of you.

From ROGERS Radio: Peter McKeown, Rick Doughty, James Dahlke, Dan Hunt and Jamie O'Connell, Andy Wilson, Dean Belanger, Amber Livingstone, Cathy Vossos, Patty Garlick, Dave Certossi, Richard Coffin, Bob Coles, David Sheridan, Mitch Belanger, Nancy Slater, Holly Congiano and Kevin Oschefski - you have all helped make this book and this dream possible. You are all very much appreciated.

From The Nugget: Dan Johnson, Steve Page, Julie Perry, Jim Hutchison, Jennifer Hamilton-McCharles, Cheryl Archer, Anthony Ricciuti, Jayme Madore, Lucy South, Andrea Coxford, Mel Billings and Chris Kelly - thank you for your professionalism and fun.

From CTV: Ron Driscoll, Connie Guindon, Linda Holmes, Shawn Croteau and Kevin "the intern" - you are all so easy and pleasant to work with.

From Blue Sky Radio: Kristin Shepherd, Natalie Lucier, Jamie Littlejohn, and Valerie Gow - you are a team of caring and dedicated souls.

From COGECO Cable: Brian Winkworth and Greg Estabrooks.

From The MOOSE Radio: Mike Monaghan.

From BayToday.ca: Kate Adams

From the staff at Creative Impressions: Ron Laplante, Sue Barr, Jessie Charette, Joanne Seeburger, Mike Snyder, Merv and Tom and the bindery and graphics department.

From the "friends we can't live without" list - Paul Barton, Bruce Barton, Barb Drenth, Kayleigh Drenth, Penny Tremblay, and Ava Vosu, thank you for your willingness to share your stories and bare your souls on the TV commercials - we are eternally grateful.

To Nancy Fischer for her genius at event planning and the You`re My Hero Publicity Manual she created; Marion Cook, of BMO, a constant cheerleader and dear friend of Karen and Barry; and John McLellan of Tim Hortons who is helping spread the Hero message – our thanks and appreciation.

Tim Spilchuk, Salvatore Pullara, Monique Lugli, Maria Speth and Jim Seguin, for their advice and good wishes.

Our Mayor Vic Fedeli, our MP Anthony Rota, Gregory Kolz in Mr. Rota's office, our MPP Monique Smith and her staff members, Melissa Zanette and Jason Corbett, we thank all of you for your blushing praise and sincere support of this book and our dream.

Bette Daoust, a Canadian living in San Francisco, has been "waving the flag" for this project right from the beginning.

Bette wants to duplicate what we have done in North Bay - all over the USA. You are a blessing, Bette. Thank you for your advice and caring.

Shannon Parish, of Denver Colorado, who felt compelled to draw a cartoon family for You're My Hero; Master Videographer, Eric Boutilier from Flic Media; John Delaplaine and Steve Shane of Delaplaine Creative for their innovative, intricate and brilliant web design; Greg Brewer for his awesome design of our logo; North Bay native, Randy Thomson, for his trust-inspiring legal work; Joe Sinclair, a steadying influence for the expansion of this dream - thank you all for your professionalism.

Lauri Petz, Lorna Jenkins, Gail Malden, Peter Chirico, Don Silveri and Paul Barton of the Royal Bank of Canada - your support and enthusiasm are much appreciated.

We thank Patti Carr, Sue Adams and their team at the North Bay and District Chamber of Commerce for their constant and never-ending support of our work.

Many thanks to Kelly Peer-Ranger and Charles Elliott of TD - Canada Trust and Alice Radley of P.H.A.R.A. who graciously allowed us to speak to their teams about heroes in the workplace.

Many thanks to Erin Richmond, Nicole Truman, Karen Jones and all of the Small Business Success Office team at City Hall in North Bay.

Thank you to my original coauthors and mentors from the Chicken Soup for the Soul® books: Jack Canfield, Mark Victor Hansen and Patty Aubery – your love, kindness, and caring helped me become a better businessperson and a better man.

Our generous sponsors have made it possible for us to do something that no one has ever done before, (to our knowledge): give 50% of the selling price of each book to charities and not-for-profit groups. We encourage our readers to support and acknowledge these community-minded businesses.

A huge thank you to Paul Lamont and Derek Shogren of Canadian Tire. They are true heroes and champions of charitable causes in North Bay. They have helped so many charities in our area. When they found out that $10.00 of each book sold will be going to charity, they agreed to become the main distribution outlet for this book.

Our sincere appreciation goes to Danny Guenette and his team at STAPLES: Pat Lynch, Norm Desrosier, Derek MacFarlane, and Ken Gervais. You have a wonderful store and an amazing staff!

Mary-Jo and Michel Racine have been long-time friends and supporters. When the "bell rang" to help in the final stages of this book, they both showed up and helped us to the finish line.

When you are considering someone to co-author a book like this - the next phase of my life's work - it is important to pick someone who you trust and someone who cares about people. When Penny Tremblay agreed to be my co-author, a smile came to my face and a peace came to my heart because I knew that our project was in good hands. One of her greatest assets will be the promotion of the book through her authentic, caring presence. Where Penny goes, people want to follow. She is a wonderful leader, a smart businessperson, and a dear friend. Thank you so much, Penny. I wish you the best!

Laura Little is one of the most patient and loving graphic artists and typesetters I have ever met. Laura's calming influence allowed us to be creative, stir things up and make mistakes. All we would ever hear from Laura was, "Whatever you need to make this project the best, I'll do it." Laura, you are a blessing!

What do you call someone who is smart, funny, talented, trusting, loving, direct, a good salesperson, an advocate for what is right and noble, and a dear friend? We call her Carolyn Samuel. Carolyn asked Barry to come in to her night school English class and share with the students, the Chicken Soup story and the You're My Hero story. Three hours later the janitor was knocking on the door saying, "we're closing up now." Carolyn became a fan of the project and its ideals right away. She eventually became the senior editor for the book and has personally read, edited, massaged, and loved every story. Everyone who picks up this book and is touched by it can thank Carolyn for her role as an angel in the completion of this book.

Finally, to Karen Spilchuk - your support of me is unparalleled: support as a wife, co-parent, partner, cheerleader, confidant, and best friend. I love you so much. Thank you for your constant belief in me. Other than God and my parents, I know of no other person in the world who would have stuck by me through all the dreams, all the hopes, and all the lessons we have learned and shared together. Thank you - is not enough. I love you - is close. Thank you Heavenly Father for my wife - is it. Amen.

DID YOU KNOW?

Your generosity of time, effort and money has allowed us to make a donation of
$8.00 - $10.00
for each book sold to local charities.

LOCAL SCHOOLS
If you purchased your book at a school, the donation stays with them to support school projects.

NIPISSING WOMEN'S TRANSITION HOUSE
If you purchased your book at Canadian Tire or from Barry Spilchuk, the donation is given to Nipissing Women's Transition House.

REWARD!!!
WANTED - YOUR EAGLE EYES

Be on the lookout for: spelling mistakes, typos, incorrect page numbers, improper grammar, oversights, and missed names.

Despite the heroic efforts of our team, we realize that we may have made a mistake or two along the way. We would love your help and input. If you find an error, please e-mail us.

As a **REWARD** for your help we will send you an e-copy of our article entitled:

THE 12 KEYS TO PROSPERITY

Please send an e-mail and tell us what the error is and what page it is on: **oops@ymhbooks.com**

Thank you for being part of the You're My Hero™ team!

PERSONAL DEDICATION

My Ultimate Hero,
SOPHIE SORON

*Barry and his grandma, Sophie Soron,
at the Toronto Blue Jay's game on
her 92nd birthday - April 2007.*

TABLE OF CONTENTS

Chapter One: Our Everyday Heroes

Chapter Two: Our Friends

Chapter Six: Our Grade Ones

Chapter Seven: Our Military

Chapter Eight: Our Grandmothers

Chapter Nine: Our Grandfathers

Chapter Ten: Our Celebrated Heroes

Chapter Eleven: Heroes In Our Schools

Chapter Twelve: Our Families

Chapter Thirteen: Our Grade Threes and Fours

Hero Highlights from our Terrific Threes and Fantastic Fours

Chapter Fourteen: Our Community

Chapter Fifteen: Our Hero Within

Our Generous Sponsors

INTRODUCTION

By co-author,
Penny Tremblay

As a consultant, trainer and motivator for over 15 years, I have learned that there is tremendous value in leadership skills - some of the most important ones being communication and relationship-building.

To thrive, succeed, and be happy in our own lives, we need others. We need strong relationships in both our personal and professional lives. The most important social graces that we can use to build a foundation for great rapport and relationships are acknowledgement, recognition, and the ability to show sincere appreciation.

You're My Hero™ Books is a concept that does just that. It encourages people to share their love and appreciation, to acknowledge the efforts of those who have made a difference in their lives, and to exercise gratitude for that which they have received.

It is a clever concept with a heart-driven purpose; I commend Barry and Karen Spilchuk for the opportunity that they have extended to this community. We have already benefited by learning to be grateful for the generous acts of others and by practicing and exercising our literacy skills. This is just the beginning of a new revolution of reading, fundraising, and becoming our personal best as contributors and readers.

Inside, you will read stories of everyday heroism and how it has affected the lives of so many writers. From friends saving caterpillars and teddy bears from the lake, to a teacher making a life-altering difference in a youth's path, to the souls who have passed, who can no longer be praised in person for their value and importance, you will learn lessons of life, love, appreciation, and acknowledgment and how significant they all are.

Selecting a hero to write about is a difficult task when we start to think of all of the options and people who have made a difference to each of us individually. There are many choices: parents, grandparents, relatives, whether they are living or no longer with us, teachers, neighbours, citizens within our community … the list is long.

The lesson is that, no matter your age, the rest of your life is ahead of you - to build successful relationships, live a happy life and honour those in your life who make a difference. It simply contributes to the happiness of others and it bounces right back to you in the form of joy. You reap what you sow.

I would like to dedicate this book to all of the contributors. Whether your story was selected for publication, or your name and hero's name appear on the Honour Roll, or you have purchased a copy to support a charity, you have made a valuable contribution. I commend you for your recognition of someone or some organization that has made an impact on our society in a positive way.

People are creatures of emotion, sometimes motivated by pride and vanity. People won't always remember what you taught them or what you've told them, but people will always remember how you made them feel.

Life is short, shorter for some than others. May this book enrich your life and empower you to continue making recognition and acknowledgement a part of your day. Catch people doing things right and commend them, verbally or publicly, for their efforts. Show gratitude for both everyday and extraordinary efforts made by the people around you, for life is as much about giving as it is about receiving.

Let's get started...

CHAPTER ONE

OUR EVERYDAY HEROES

It often happens that those of whom we speak least on earth are best known in heaven.

Nicolas Caussin

The Unnoticed Heroes

What is a hero? Is it a fictional character, with superhuman abilities, that goes around saving the world from evil? Welcome to the media-corrupt version of the definition, making it impossible to compare to modern-day men and women. What abilities do they possess that make them worthy of that title? How can someone, in this reality, compete?

A single mother, at a minimum-wage job, works her hands to the bone to feed a starving family because she has no education. Not only because she couldn't afford it at that time, but because she believed she didn't need it. Why would she? She loved her husband, not enough to stop him from walking out, obviously, but maybe if she was a superhero, she could have prevented that. Maybe. No, she's ignored. Her children can't see how hard she works. It had to be her fault their father walked out. She's not a hero.

What about the teachers who make it their life's work to teach others what they have learned? They strive to give an education to those who want one and, more so, to those who don't. They try to help them see something inside themselves that nobody else can. A teacher sees potential in a teenager, born into a welfare family, who spends every hour at his dead-end job trying to earn enough cash for another row of cocaine. The teacher spends time trying to turn that teen into somebody he doesn't want to be and who will, undoubtedly, be sent to an early grave before the ink on his final transcript is dry. That teacher can't be a hero.

She tried, giving hours of attention to the teen, but nobody sees that. She's just doing her job, right?

My heroes are the misunderstood. Those that I've just stated and those who are like those I just stated, yet on a smaller scale. The ones who put themselves before others and are never noticed - or when they are, it's nothing special. My heroes are those who don't consider themselves heroes yet are in every way, whether they display the qualities needed or not. The misunderstood, the unheard, and the ones who go for what is morally and ethically correct, versus the society-censored version. They're all around me, sometimes. They deserve at least that much said about them.

Matt St. Onge

CHAPTER TWO

OUR FRIENDS

A friend is a single soul dwelling in two bodies.

Aristotle

Amy DeGenova
(Rain to Remember)

A year ago, I made the great journey from Chelny, Russia, to North Bay. I met many interesting people in Canada. Everyone was curious about me at first, asking the same questions: who I am, where I am from, how do I like the country, and so on. But as quickly as I could answer their questions, they were forgetting about me, my thoughts, and how I felt. They did not want to deal with the foreigner experiencing the tribulations of a new language in a new country.

It was hard to live around people who did not understand me as much as I did not understand them. I felt lonely - no - isolated. Amy DeGenova was the one who made a difference in my life. I can't even imagine how much patience she needed to keep trying to explain the things she wanted to tell or ask me. She was the one who did not only ask me all those kinds of questions, but also helped me around. She helped me to survive in a new society.

I remember the first time I slept over at Amy's house. We went for a walk at night. She asked me a simple question, "How late does your mother let you stay out at night in Russia?" That question sounds simple to any English-speaking person, but back then, I could hardly understand any part of it. "How your mother you night in Russia". That's how it sounded to me. They were the only words I could understand. I couldn't figure out what she was trying to say. I felt silly because I could not understand simple things. She started explaining to me the question. "How long..." she started, pointing at her wrist, "does your mother", she added and I nodded, showing her that I understood that part. Actually, all I could recognize was the word 'mother'. "Let you stay out..." she continued, stopping her walk, "at night", she finished by gesturing to the sky in an attempt to explain the word 'night'. I stared at her with a huge smile on my face, trying to decipher what she was trying to say. "Do you understand?" she asked finally. "No" was all I could say, swinging my head.

I was doing my best to understand her, but I couldn't. I didn't want to disappoint her, but all her diligence was for nothing. She smiled to me and said, "It's okay". We continued to walk. It started raining. To keep up our conversation, I asked her, "What is it?" I turned a palm skyward, letting the droplets fall into it. "It's rain," she answered politely. "Rain," I repeated thoughtfully, lifting my arms and my head up and looking at the lowering sky. It was my new learned word for the night. She smiled to me with her warm and gentle smile. "Let's get running or we will be dripping wet by the time we get home." I caught a familiar word, "run", and I understood what she wanted us to do.

A year passed by. My English has improved a lot since then. Both of us will remember that night. When it's raining outside and I am looking on the rain through my window, I know somewhere my best friend is looking through the window also, thinking of me. We gave each other a promise.

Luba Dushnitskaya, 18

Barb Weeks
(Restoring My Faith)

I stand here…my four-year-old son tightly clutching my hand. I am nervous, agitated, embarrassed, and excited. Yes, it is true that I am excited, but the other emotions overwhelm me and I must search for that part of me that knows this is right; knows that this is something I can and must do. So many thoughts and emotions swirl around and through me as I step through the doorway. My son is asking questions and says he likes the colourful poster on the wall. Oh, to be a child once more.

There is someone in the classroom; I thought it would be empty. The woman turns, smiles, and comes my way. My palms begin to sweat and my son squeezes tighter. The woman comes across the room in record time and as her eyes meet mine, I lower my head and look down at the floor. Within minutes, this woman somehow manages to make me feel welcome and safe, and I lift my eyes and meet her smile. This was the first time I met my hero. This woman was a teacher in the Adult Education Program and she was soon to be teacher, mentor and friend.

One week after our initial meeting, I slunk into the classroom, carefully choosing a seat at the back of the class; somewhere where I could remain invisible amongst the other students in the class. I watched this woman welcome us, encourage us, laugh with us, share with us, and I knew she loved being in this room. I, on the other hand, did not love being in this room…not yet.

Two weeks after our initial meeting, this woman came to me - she had noticed me regardless of my attempts at invisibility - and told me we needed to talk. I was mortified. What could she want? Is she going to tell me I am not smart enough? Is she going to say I do not belong here? Is she going to ask me to leave the class?

This woman told me I did not belong here. After 16 years of being out of school, I had registered in grade 10 courses. She definitely thought I did not belong here - I belonged in a much more advanced course. What? How could this be? My ex-husband spent the last five years of my life telling me over and over how stupid I was; why does this cheerful, smiling, intelligent woman think I am so capable? I was confused.

After serious deliberation, I made a decision: I was going to trust this woman. That was years ago. The woman's name is Barb Weeks. She is my hero.

After many years in an intense marriage, I managed to escape with my three children and start a new life. It was a slow process and a terrifying one. As I had been separated from family and friends for over five years, isolated into the world of my ex-husband, I became a shell of my former self. My confidence was stripped. I was afraid for my children and myself; what did our futures hold? I no longer knew the person I once was.

Going back to school had always been my dream, not his. Now I had the chance and I had to do it. Even though I felt so terrible about myself, I knew I must do this to prove to myself that I was capable, to prove to him that he was wrong and, most importantly, to be self-sufficient and able to take care of my children. If I had not met Barb Weeks at this time in my life, I honestly wonder where I would be today.

Perhaps I would still be a teacher and have a wonderful career, a great family and a close group of friends. Perhaps I would be waitressing and barely making ends meet. Perhaps...perhaps....perhaps...

Barb encouraged me, befriended me, believed in me, guided me, and became my mentor. She never judged. She took my hand and dragged me to university. She was at my graduation. She acted as my reference for my first teaching interview and, with her help, I got the job! She retired and gifted me with her resources, her guidance, and her happiness for me. In return, I became the person I once was. I became a strong individual, an excellent student, a powerful role model for my children, and an independent single mother with a fabulous career.

With Barb, together we took down the wall that surrounded my being and allowed the fresh air and the sunshine to come through. With the destruction of the prison I had built around myself, came freedom for all of us: my children, my family, and our futures.

When I heard Barb was ill, I cried for her pain. I felt like it was my own mother. I prayed for her; my children and I talked about her and thought about her each and every day. In true Barb fashion, she beat her illness and became an even larger lover of life, which I would not have believed possible before.

Barb is now my friend. We are in the same book club and every meeting or conversation we have is a joy for me. Each time I see her or talk to her, I feel young, alive, and full of possibilities. I share every occasion and milestone with her. I share my children's graduations and celebrations with Barb.

Last night I delighted in telling her that I was getting married. Oh, how wonderful it is to have her to share my happiness with. She hugged me and said, "Wow! I am so happy for you! I know where you came from and I have watched you come full circle. This is so fabulous! It must restore your faith in ...everything."

That statement is close, but it is not quite accurate. It was you, Barb, who restored my faith in everything. One day at a time, you restored my faith. Through your kindness, your devotion, your nonjudgmental belief in me, your love of life, your strength in the face of illness, your excited responses to all of my news, and your very presence in my life - you restored my faith. From the moment you saw me standing in the door with my four-year-old son, eyes to the ground, head and shoulders stooped, you believed in me. That was 14 years ago. The woman's name is Barb Weeks. She is my hero.

Lynda Marshall

Jerri Clout
(The Girl Who Did)

I remember all the days that I would run up the driveway and knock on my neighbour's door. Maureen would answer and have a big smile on her face, welcoming me in. I would rush up the stairs looking for her, searching high and low, "Jerri? Jerri? Where are you?" and then she would pop up and we would both giggle.

Whenever I look into my past, I see her, my best friend, and every day we'd forget about the world and just have fun. We would sit at the computer and make cartoons or use paper maché to make piggy banks. We'd see each other almost every, single day and we would always find something to do, but when school came along, it was a different story. I had to move across town and wouldn't be able to run up her driveway every day, whenever I wanted to see her. It was a hard time to let go. We still had play dates, but it wasn't the same.

As the years passed, we'd always invite each other to our birthdays and it would be the best times of the year. Just a few years ago, I noticed a newspaper article about Jerri. She was helping fundraise to fight certain diseases, and organizing walks to help cure them. I was so impressed, so amazed, and so happy for her that I didn't even know what to say. My best friend was becoming famous!

One morning I woke up, turned on the radio and, lo and behold, my best friend was discussing all of her accomplishments for the fight against HIV/AIDS. I couldn't believe that the girl I've known my whole life could go out into the world, head on, and fight for what she believed in. I was so proud to say I knew her and whenever I said her name to my friends, it was always an honour.

I believe she is one of the nicest, most thoughtful people in the world. She doesn't worry about herself, or what people think of her. She goes out and does what she believes in. Jerri wants to change the world. She once invited me to join a baseball team with her and now, six years later, I am still playing, still throwing, catching and hitting the ball, all because Jerri thought that I would have fun playing a sport with her during the summer.

Last year, I received a letter from Jerri in the mail, asking if I would be interested in putting up some posters around my school to raise awareness about Patrick4Life, a local walk/run that she was helping to organize. Once again, that girl seemed to amaze me. She goes out and spends her spare time helping others. It's inspirational! I jumped at the chance to help her, by putting up posters around my school.

A few weeks ago, my teacher was looking for volunteers at Chippewa to help out with this year's Patrick4Life campaign. I immediately thought of my best friend, Jerri, and raised my hand and said, "I'LL DO IT, I'LL DO IT!" I plan on making that one of the first steps to achieving my goal.

If there is one thing in life that I want to accomplish someday, it is that I want to be just as thoughtful, just as outgoing, and just as nice as Jerri is and to be remembered as someone who made a difference in our community.

Maggie Daniel, 15

Scott and Cheryl Clark

All I remember is feeling joyful and festive. To this day, I don't know how a responsible adult manages to get herself caught in such a ridiculous position, but there I was, awkwardly straddling a wire fence in fabulous wedge shoes, at one o'clock in the morning. It was a long drop, and it could have proven to be an excruciating one if it hadn't been for my dearest buddy, Scott Clark. He was the Heritage Festival chair and I was a volunteer on the entertainment committee. On his 40th birthday, he, myself, and another friend of his, managed to get locked in the park after hours and were left alone to climb out. It was one of those truly fun memories, the kind that gets made when you allow yourself to appreciate a moment as it's happening.

I don't think that's how most people would open a hero story about Scottie. I could discuss his extensive charitable work. It's estimated that he's helped various groups, such as the Santa Fund, raise more than $500,000. Then there's the remarkable contributions he's made as president of Benjamin James Marketing and Communications. He's accomplished so much, including winning the Kiwanis Citizen of the Year, since his 14 years as North Bay's premiere morning man on EZ Rock. But in the end, none of it matters, at least not to me.

The thing about Scottie and his wife, Cheryl, that has touched me the most, is the general feeling of positivity and warmth they convey to those around them. I'm happy if

I see them coming towards me and, after a brief conversation, I feel uplifted when I walk away. They actually get what it means to cast away the bad, focus on the good, and forge ahead with optimism. It's a way of life I hold dear and I enjoy having these working examples to look up to.

As a young woman who eventually wants to start a family, I look at Cheryl and wonder if I will be able to accomplish what she does in a day. She too has quite an impressive resume. She's a working mother of two, a supportive wife, a community-oriented citizen and the life of every hot tub party she's ever hosted. She embodies fun. I often wonder if she understands the profound admiration she draws, all on her own, in her infectious, not-so-quiet way. I've gone on a couple of walks with her in the past and discussed books and family and the like. I became partial to her realism and heart-felt humanity.

On one of those strolls along the waterfront with Cheryl, she told me that Scott was not actually from North Bay but from Scarborough. I was surprised and impressed because, out of all the times I bumped into him, whether it was when I was a reporter for The Nugget and he was on the radio, or later during the Nipissing Stage Company years, he carried himself with the dedication and passion of someone born and bred in our little Hockeyville.

Many people could have written a hero story about Scott and Cheryl Clark. Whenever their names are mentioned, they are always followed by complimentary remarks. I'm not embellishing when I say that I've never met anyone who didn't respect or admire this couple. For all the compassion both of you have shown, the time you have invested, and the warmth you bring, I want you to know that North Bay loves you back. You make a positive impact every day and have made a remarkable impression on me. Thank you for your generous spirits.

Carolyn Samuel

Shawn Venasse
(An Extraordinary Hairy Duck)

He's known as the guy who will give you as many high-fives as the days of the month. He'll give you rides on elevators and wheelchair ramps. All of the parabus drivers know him. He's the one you must honk for, if you pass him. To his close and personals, he is known as the Hairy Duck, a.k.a. Shawn Venasse.

For those who don't know Shawn, let me tell you about him. Shawn was born on July 22nd, 1982, along with his twin brother, Steven, to Michael and Lori Venasse. Shawn was born with cerebral palsy but that, of course, never stops him. He can swim 30 laps in a pool, has been on a plane, and up the CN tower. He has been to Florida. He is a big brother to a little brother and two little sisters, and he is a big fan of roller coasters.

Shawn does some pretty cool things for the disabled community in North Bay. Not only is he a great role model for the NADY (Nipissing Association for Disabled Youth), and a great participator, but he brings out the best in everyone.

I met Shawn through his little sister, Laura, a best friend of mine. I completely fell in love with his personality and spunk. He taught me not to be nervous around disabled kids and now I am one of his counselors at NADY.

Shawn brings out the most amazing parts in everyone with his kind spirit and amazing qualities. When you make him smile, you immediately have to grin, too, because every smile you get from Shawn is something that means a lot. He also gives great hugs. He is self-accepting and sees the good in everyone and he will never judge you. He can bring even the most eccentric of people back down to earth with his personality. He is full of unconditional love.

Anyone who meets Shawn is drawn to him right away. You cannot be in a bad mood around Hairy Duck. When I'm around him, no matter what my mood, he immediately picks me up, especially when he calls me Bobby, the nickname he gave me. I'm greeted with, "Hi, Bobby! How are you today?" My Hairy Duck is an extraordinary guy!

Abby Cook, 17

Emily Gough
(Emily's New Lungs)

She was the bravest person I had ever met. She just accepted the fact that she was sick and that was all she could really do. Emily Gough was one of my best friends but, unfortunately, she passed away on February 17th, 2006.

She went to Toronto's Sick Kids' Hospital in 2002, where she patiently waited for a double-lung transplant. She was getting sicker and sicker by the day with Cystic Fibrosis. Back at school, even though our hope and faith were strong, we did not know if she was going to make it. But one day, she got the phone call that changed her life. She was getting new lungs! We were so happy that we were going to get to see her the following year in grade eight.

The summer blew by and, soon enough, I got off the bus and saw her standing there. It had been such a long time since I had last seen her. We had a transplant party for her on November 2nd, 2005, celebrating the fact that she had new lungs for one whole year.

Time rolled on to the last time I saw her. One morning, she came in from outside and she was crying really hard. She was saying that her legs were sore and that she couldn't walk. Another girl and I helped her to the office. Later that week, we got the news that Emily was back at Sick Kids' because her body was rejecting the new lungs. That's why her legs were so sore.

That Friday, I was coming home from a dance when my father told me that she had passed away earlier that day. I was devastated and so upset. The second I got in the door, I called my teacher and we talked for awhile. It really helped because she explained to me that Emily could now run, for the first time in her life, without having trouble breathing and she didn't have to take pills anymore and that she was, finally, perfectly healthy. No one was happy that she had passed but we knew she wouldn't suffer anymore. She was a great person who inspired many people. I know she will always be with me, even if it is just in spirit.

Katie Forth, 15

Tracy Kennedy

I was so excited to be spending some time in my favorite community. It had been our home for eight years. As we reached Espanola, we stopped at our favorite pit stop, Wendy's, and got something to eat. Soon we would be in Elliot Lake.

Every summer, I return to visit good friends and stay with my best friend, Tracy Kennedy. Like always, as we pulled up in front of Tracy's house, she was watching out the living room window. She came running out the front door and we greeted with big smiles and warm hugs. Once inside and after hellos and hugs for Chris and Tom, our parents visited out on the deck. My mom and dad told Chris and Tom about a seizure I had had a week ago, my very first. I had gone to the hospital and was checked out. Appointments were made for me to see a doctor in two months. Tracy and I went upstairs to catch up, talked about school, sports and Canada Day celebrations. Ever since we were little, we had always gone to the big beach party. July 1st arrived and we woke up to a rainy day. The beach party was being rescheduled for July 2nd. It was a day that would change my life, my family's life, and the lives of all those close to me, including my best friend.

After many activities to celebrate Canada's birthday, it was time to go home. Tracy and I packed up all of our stuff and walked back to Tracy's house. When we arrived home there was a note along with 20 dollars. "Tracy, if you and Abeba clean the van, you girls can split the 20 dollars. See you soon, love Chris and Tom." We agreed it was a great deal. I was feeling hot and tired and just needed to rest for awhile. I decided I would go float on the air mattress in Tracy's small pool. It felt good and was so relaxing. Tracy came out and had everything ready to clean the van. I just needed a few more minutes. She went inside and, a short time later, came out and called for me, but saw me nowhere in the yard. After looking around, Tracy describes this moment as knowing something was terribly wrong. She walked towards the pool and there she saw me, on the bottom, curled up in a ball. Tracy jumped in, pulled me out of the pool, and placed me on the lawn. She administered CPR, something she had learned in her babysitter's course a few years back.

I began coughing and spitting. And then I was breathing, Tracy cleared my airway as there was blood. She then ran inside and dialed 911, trying to stay calm in what was a frightening situation. She gave the woman her address and told her what had happened. The ambulance soon arrived. It took several hours before the nurses and doctors had me stable enough for the helicopter ride to Sudbury General Hospital. My parents, now back in North Bay, had been notified and they set off for Sudbury to be there when I arrived. The Kennedys, my sisters, and other close friends all made their way to Sudbury that night. Over the next week, I was on life-support, kept on an ice bed to help prevent any brain damage, and was in an induced coma.

My family and friends stayed with me, taking turns every minute of the day. Tracy was there, through it all. Due to complications with my trachea and not being able to breathe, they gave me a tracheotomy, but only for a short time. When I awoke from the coma, my parents and sisters, along with Tracy, Chris, and Tom, welcomed me back. Tracy had brought me a writing board so that I could communicate. My first words that I wrote were, "Thank you, Tracy, for saving my life and, to Chris and Tom, thank you for always putting up with me. I love you all dearly."

It has taken a long time to recover from this accident, but I am well now. I take medication twice a day for epilepsy and I have to follow many safety measures. My friends at school all know what to do if I have a seizure. On May 17th, 2007, my family and I went to Sudbury and attended an awards ceremony. Tracy received an award for her bravery from the Ontario Provincial Police, as well as from Saint John's Ambulance. It was a great night, to see my hero recognized for saving my life. This is dedicated to Tracy Kennedy, my sister. Loving you always - Tracy & Abeba re-united, August 2007.

Abeba Kitchen, 16

Amy Hurtubise

It started about two years ago when I found myself sitting on the field, writing in a little red notebook. "Hey" was all it took for me to tilt my head up and reply, "Hi." I had never really taken the time to talk to her before, but suddenly I found myself wanting to know more. After that day, we spent lots of time together being the best of friends. Many people can say they're best friends with someone. It can mean a lot or nothing at all. In this case, I'm pretty sure it means everything. I have never had a friend who was so nice, who treated me with such respect, and who I could tell absolutely everything to, without worrying that it would get around to others.

We spent our time sitting in the snow in the winter, hanging out at each other's houses in the fall, enjoying the sun in the spring, and spending time with friends during the summer. We went to the beach, sat on my deck, ate popsicles, and drank Diet Pepsi. We were the friends that could have two-hour conversations about nothing, laugh about the most stupid and pointless things, and never get annoyed with each other. Although we've always had different interests, she had a huge impact on my life and taught me things I probably never would've known if I didn't know her.

She's been there when I've needed to talk and always supported my decisions. She's had an honest opinion on everything, whether it is a boy, my favorite shirt, or what I would be doing on the weekend.

We have never really had a big fight. We've had little arguments, but we'd always find ourselves laughing at whatever we said, or did, two minutes after it happened. Or in my case, running out of the room and yelling at her and then coming back with something to eat and saying, "Here, you want one?", knowing it wouldn't be worth staying mad. She was there through hard times when I thought I'd never want to talk to anyone ever again.

Although I haven't always approved of her decisions, I wouldn't stop her from doing the things she wanted, unless it was serious. We couldn't stop each other from living our lives the way we've wanted to. She's always been by my side. At the start of high school, at Chippewa, we were still pretty close. As our lives progressed and school went on, things got harder and we made new friends. We had already begun to drift apart, regardless of how much we didn't want to. Just recently, we have stopped being the same. We're still friends, just not as much as in the beginning. I know she's still there for me and I'm still here for her. I could never hate that girl or find myself not wanting to be around her. She's had a major impact on my life and that's all I want her to know.

Tayler Allison, 14

Zack Mullin

(Your Voice was the Soundtrack of my Summer)

Zack Christopher Mullin doesn't know what he's done for me. To those who know either of us, they would never expect to be reading this. Truthfully, they would probably laugh. To many he is just a punk, a kid who has no direction in life and one whom adults would rather shun than embrace. His extraordinary talents are hidden underneath the tough image he emulates. The Zack Mullin that inspires me exhibits a true sense of reality, always questioning views and ideas with a maturity and wisdom far beyond his years.

He's never had it easy. He's the oldest of four other siblings and grew up in Sudbury's ghetto, using the sport of wrestling as an outlet for his anger. This is how I met him. We were shoved onto the same bus as 3000 athletes cleared out of the opening ceremonies for the 2006 Ontario Winter Games. A figure skater and a wrestler make an unlikely, yet perfect, combination.

There was something different about him from the moment I caught his eye. We exchanged e-mails and, a few weeks later, we were talking on the phone every day. These were not the traditional phone conversations one might assume. Moving here at the age of nine, it took me two years to begin to make true friends. I had already become extremely self-conscious and shy. I've always been a curious person, but every time I began to talk about certain topics, I was made fun of, so I stopped right away, in my feeble attempt to be accepted. After that, my mind got so wrapped up in self-absorbing, high school drama that I had shut it off to all its intellectual capabilities. Finally, I had someone to relate to. Zack shared with me his theories about the universe, religion, politics, and reality. He shared these with ease and confidence. In turn, I naturally began to question my own. I had never felt so alive! His voice and questions unlocked the door and reopened my mind. He taught me not to fear what other people think of you, and slowly gave me my self-confidence back. Having it back again feels awfully refreshing.

I feel so empowered when I express my views on a subject that I am passionate about. Being able to convince another person to trust in your belief or reasoning is an absolutely indescribable sensation. Something about him makes me want to change myself, to change the world, to do something really meaningful and purposeful with my life. It is hard for me to admit it, but I love him. I love him more than I thought I could ever love a person. He has helped me through the most difficult situations I've ever had to go through within these 17 years. His voice was the only thing that stopped my tears during the entire spring and summer of 2006.

A year later, I am so much more aware of my surroundings. He has helped me realize and come to terms with my beliefs and morals in life. My family and friends may not appreciate or admire who I've become, but Zack helped me rid myself of what I hated most in life: who I was. With all of the doors he has helped to open for me, I hope someday I can make such a profound impact on the world that I make him proud.

Erin Bros, 17

Charlotte Smith

In the early 1940s, I lived in a rural area. I was able to take grades nine and ten in a one-room, country school. Grade 11 was taken care of by my parents, taking a small apartment in town for the winter. Grade 12 posed a problem as there was no school bus service. This meant going to the nearest centre to board. My mother inquired at the high school and was given the name of a Charlotte Smith who would take a student, at a dollar a day for room and board. By today's standards, that seems incredibly reasonable, but five dollars a week in cash was hard to come by.

Charlotte Smith lived in a two-storey home in the central core of the town. At that time, she had another girl boarding with her and two girls of her own at home. She was a remarkable woman. Later she told us that, before her marriage, her husband told her they wouldn't have a family as she was thought to be too delicate. Instead, they had 10 children, six boys and four girls. Her husband died before the last girl was born. Charlotte was left to steer six boys through their teen years during the depression days. Five grew to be worthy citizens. Tragedy struck, though, as one boy died of spinal meningitis just as he was reaching adulthood.

At the time I boarded there, World War II was on and the family dispersed into the services. Some were married by then. I was an only child and not used to a large family.

When they came home on leave, they would tease me by asking, "Shirley, what is the word for today," indicating that I was a quiet one.

Mrs. Smith had had an accident, while chopping wood when she was young, and had one glass eye. It was a good match but it fascinated us. She was a Christian woman, a devout Baptist. She belonged to a missionary society. Once, for a program they were having on Bolivia, they used jelly beans for currency which they called Bolivianos. I always think of this when I see jelly beans.

Busy as she was, she always celebrated birthdays. For my 17th birthday, she crocheted a blue necklace that rolled into a twisted rope. She also did bows for our hair that fastened in with bobby pins. Of course, there was cake too.

Sometimes, we would hurry home from school and, after a quick lunch, managed a hand or two of bridge before returning to school. A special meal was shared when the Italian neighbour across the road brought over a pasta dish. I stayed two years with Mrs. Smith and, after more than 60 years, still have casual contact with her daughter.

Shirley Demaine

Christina Hinds

It was the first day at M.T. Davidson. I was in grade six and knew practically no one. One afternoon, I was washing my hands in the school bathroom. The sinks at M.T. Davidson weren't the easiest to operate so, while I was dancing around trying to make it work, Christina came over and stepped on the bar that turns on the water. Being a little embarrassed, I just thanked her. Within the next couple of weeks, we became inseparable.

I remember almost every weekend, going over to her house and playing Beenie Babies (we usually never played but instead built them houses). For us, it was so much fun. Then, in grade seven, we started going to the mall all the time. If we weren't at one of our houses, we were at the mall. We did, and still do, so many stupid things. We used to have a band with no instruments, just Christina and I, called Kidilicious. Also, we used to wear the same clothes and everyone thought we were twins. Most people still do.

Even if I just wanted to get rid of Christina, I couldn't. Our fights only last two minutes before we get bored of not talking. Now we are in grade nine at West Ferris Secondary School and I am so glad that I have Christina. I hope that we stay friends until the end.

Brittany Inthof, 14

CHAPTER THREE

OUR MOMS

The tie which links mother and child is of such pure and immaculate strength as to be never violated.

Washington Irving

Kathryn (Kathy) Sirrs
(Flowers of Life)

At the beginning of the 1990's, my mom had no husband, no kids, and was sad and lonely. She had desperately wanted kids her entire life and, as she was 40 years old, time was ticking. Artificial insemination turned out to be the answer. After only two attempts and nine months, I was born. Six months after that, she married my dad, and three years later my little sister, Meaghan, was born.

Life was going great for mom. Nothing could make her happier than her two girls. She was totally in love with us, totally in love with dad, and totally in love with life. But things took a turn for the worst when she was 46 years old. Mom was diagnosed with breast cancer. Meaghan and I, being six and three years old, didn't understand. I was more disappointed that our trip to Myrtle Beach would have to be cancelled so that she could go to treatment. Little did we know that cancer would be a major theme in our lives.

I grew up with my mom constantly traveling to and from Toronto for chemotherapy, radiation and counseling. Pictures I have show her with a wide variety of hairstyles, from no hair and bandanas, to wigs, to little curly strands, to her normal bushy do. Now that I think back, mom was often tired, sick and stressed... but she always did love those shopping excursions in the big city. Every single one of the pictures showed mom flashing that big smile that no one could ever forget and her actions would never show that she was so sick. She was the best mom I could ever imagine. She did everything for Meaghan and me, from taking us for shopping sprees in Toronto to just laying in bed and crying with us every night that we needed her.

After battling breast cancer on and off for 10 long years, the doctor told us that her cancer had once again returned and had spread to her liver. I thought it would be just like the other times. She would start chemo again, lose her hair, develop those sores on her mouth, but eventually get over it.

This time was different though. She was exhausted, always sick, and showed no sign of getting better. We admitted her to the local hospital and she was quickly transferred to the best cancer hospital in Canada. Even there though, the doctors told us they couldn't do anything and that she was going to die.

About a week later, her body started deteriorating. She ate only a few ice chips a day and her once very smart mind was not working properly anymore. She didn't say much when we visited her. It was like it wasn't Mom. I had never seen her like this before and it hurt to see my mom, my best friend, not able to be her normal, energetic self. But when I would ask how much she loved us, every single time, we would see that smile and she would muster the strength to say, "soooo much!" Throughout the visits she would repeat, "It's going to be okay. I know you girls are going to be fine." We quietly reassured her that we would be.

She died on April 22nd 2007, at the age of 56… with a smile on her face. Amazingly, no matter how much pain she went through, she always stayed strong. She fought so hard every day to stay alive for my sister and me and even on her last day, she was optimistic and wore a smile.

Well over 400 people attended the funeral. Her friend made a little speech using the glass half empty/half full analogy. She said that mom didn't see the glass as half empty. "This is how she saw it," her friend said. She pulled out a small vase overflowing with bright, beautiful flowers.

It's true. That was how mom saw life, laden with flowers. Since then, many people have told me what an inspiration my mom was to them. I know her memory will live on and as I share her story with the world, I only hope that she will keep inspiring people to think about the flowers in life and to keep going on, even when times are tough.

I am so grateful that I had such an amazing woman as my mom for 16 years. Even though she is not physically here, her smiling face is always in my mind and I will forever feel her gentle embrace around me, helping me to see the flowers of life.

Katelyn Sirrs, 16

Leslie Vanderburg

My mom is Leslie Vanderburg. There are so many reasons why she is my hero, but I will name only a few. Whenever I am feeling down, or if I need help, she always comes to cheer me up. When my nine fish died, one by one, I put them in a plastic bag and my mom let me keep them in my freezer. Now, you might think that's funny, but I cried for over a month!

Anyway, back to my mom. Yes, we do get into big fights. That doesn't mean I don't love her. Heroes are very precious, so I want to keep my mom healthy and active. I love my mom. Ninety-nine point nine percent of the time we help each other, and the other 0.1% is when we get into fights. My mom cares about me. If my sister and I ride our bikes to our old house, we bring walkie-talkies in case something goes wrong. She encourages me to stay active, since I love being on the computer. She does yoga every morning and night. I love how she bakes desserts since we don't like to buy desserts. She teaches me skills and tips to study or tricks to do math. That's why my mom, Leslie Vanderburg, is my hero.

Madison Freeson, 10

Nathalie Leblanc
(My Mother, My Mentor)

So far, my teenage years can be summed up as an uphill struggle to find myself. I have tried to find myself in many ways and in many places. I have tried to find myself at parties with a stomach full of beer. I have tried to find myself in short skirts and Volcom sweaters. I have tried to find myself in dance classes, muscles aching from strain. I have tried to find myself in smoke-filled basements with drug-affiliated boyfriends who never liked me as much as they liked their paraphernalia; I definitely did not find myself there.

From each experience I wandered away, drifting aimlessly through grade 9... 10.. 11. After attaining muscle injuries, plenty of hangovers and quite the assortment of clothing, I found myself. It was not in the things I had tried all those years. It was not in the material objects I had bought, nor was it in all the friends I had met. I found myself in the humble strength of my mother. For each heart-to-heart talk we have had, each argument, each day together, I could piece myself together bit-by-bit. I found myself in my mother's heart, in its honesty and in its love.

My mother's youth is incomparable to mine. My youth, one of enjoyment and pleasure, is what my mother says she is enjoying most about her life. She tells me that my youth is her second chance, a moment in which she can relive her younger years. She thanks me for being there with her, helping with groceries, visiting the library, taking the pets to the vet, being her company. She thanks me for being who I am: a strong, independent, young woman. It's these moments where I should be thanking her.

My relationship with my mother has not always been smooth. There have been years of constantly bumping heads, disagreeing, and agreeing to disagree. The struggle to find myself created many tension-filled dinners and silent car rides. For the longest time I hated my mother's morals, values, and her concrete backbone that never allowed for very much leeway. I would complain that she was not letting me be who I wanted to be. The truth is, I never really knew who I wanted to be and the reason, I have concluded, is that she has stood by my side for so long. My mother has been my provider, my protector, my umbrella during the storms, and in times, she created a fire in me that still burns today, giving me drive and determination. She has given me everything I have ever needed: a privileged life in a beautiful house on the lake, an appreciation for what I have, plenty of rides to work and school, morals and values, a backbone, the confidence to be independent, a lot of love, and, most importantly, she has taught me to take life in strides, breathe deeply, and love myself for who I am.

It is in the moments where I doubt myself or feel as though I have failed that she is there for me the most. She has taught me that in life you do not need to do anything for anybody but yourself. She has given me the strength that allows me to excel beyond anything I thought I could be. I have grown up and opened my mind to more possibilities, welcomed more challenges and all along, I have had the faith in myself that I could do it. What the greatest thing of all? She gave me a nest to sleep in, the wings with which to fly and the lessons to teach me how to soar. After I venture out on my own, I am comfortable knowing that even if she is not flying next to me, I am under her wing. My life is our adventure.

So, in those days when I feel lost in myself, I just come home. Greeting me with big blue eyes, my mother shows me love and support in many ways. From her gentle tone to her curious question, it is in her words where I find myself. When I come home, she asks, "How was your day?" and I reply, "Good, thanks Mom". I am not thanking her for asking, but for providing me with the lessons of life that have built me, toughened me up, softened my heart, made me kind, and made me who I am today.

Ashley Leblanc, 17

Cathy Laperriere

Starting from the very first book she ever read to me, I knew my mother was my hero. I loved the way she would put so much detail and thought into every single word and then look at me as if to ask for my input.

Looking back, I see how caring and passionate she was towards me, even when I wanted to keep banging the pots while she napped, or when I'd hide in the exact same spot every time we played hide and seek. Being a single parent, she did double the work, but did everything double the better.

She taught me how to be strong and independent, to stand up for what I believed in, and pushed me to accomplish even the tiniest achievement to help me work towards what I wanted out of life. She was there for every competition, every recital, and yet still tuned the world out just to be with me.

She has helped me through some huge struggles in life and has always been that shoulder to cry on, or someone to talk to in my hour of need. She is a woman who stands tall above others and makes something beautiful out of hard work, dedication, and commitment. She strives for perfection and proves that, by being an amazing parent, a confident co-worker, and a trusting friend.

She is an enormous ball of energy and she is the fuel that keeps me going through the day. When day turns to night, she's still there, letting me squeeze her hand while I watch another episode of CSI. When I close my eyes at night, I thank God that I have such an amazing mom and when I open them in the morning, I can't wait to see her huge smile, to hear her adorable laugh, and to see her energetic self dance around in her pajamas to whatever she is listening to on my IPod.

"Let's enjoy the beautiful sunset," are the words she says almost every night during the summer. She looks up at the splashing colours of pink and purple like she looks at me when she greets me every morning, as if thankful just to be vibrant and young. And now, as I sit here writing, realizing there is no way I can really sum up my mother, I think I might just go join her on the deck for that beautiful sunset.

Cassandra Laperriere

Helen Duncan

When I was about 12 years old, my mom, Helen Duncan, went through what I would call the worst six months of her life. She separated from my father after a 13-year marriage and was laid off from a job she had had for 11 years.

I don't remember much, but I recall how much pain she was in and how I couldn't do anything about it. She was at her breaking point, but managed to make me smile every day. She still took me to my out-of-town soccer tournaments and did everything for me. How she did this, I couldn't tell you.

I would be lying in bed and could hear her cry, even though I wasn't supposed to. The best thing was that she never lied to me about what was going on. She was always honest and never left me in the dark. She was determined and motivated. My mom wasn't going to sit around and do nothing.

She went back to school to become a personal support worker, graduating with a 98 percent average and getting the highest grade in Canada on her final exam. Mom really accomplished something. She got a job at Cassellholme and it fits her well. Even I have gotten involved at Cassellholme, by volunteering there. Our family hasn't broken up because she and my father are still very good friends. Mom, you're my hero.

Rhonda Duncan, 15

Tracie Galan

Supermom

All I can do is smile as you rush through the house, trampling whoever, or whatever, is in your way as you search for your blouse in a mountain of clean laundry. Grabbing your lunch and forgetting your breakfast, while you try to put on your shoes, is a morning ritual that you seem to have done for years. I look forward to hearing you yell that you love me as you run for the van realizing, for the fifth time this week, that you're late for work.

Each morning I don't forget to tell you I love you, words that seem so simple and yet, there are thousands of reasons why I say them. From when I first scraped my knee to my first broken heart, you've been the one to make all the pain go away and the one to make me feel like there's no reason to be sad. High school can be one of the cruellest places in the world with its rumours, its bullies, and its stress. Sometimes it's been so hard that I wish I never had to wake up each morning, but you've always given me the strength to stand up.

Having me at a young age, life for my mother has never been easy. Working, going to school, and raising me was a job that very few could accomplish. She ensured that I was never hungry, scared, or alone and that I always felt cared for. She taught me about nature. She showed me how to fish and to swim, and yet there's nothing I can say besides, "I love you".

You spend unlimited hours volunteering for The Cancer Society, The Girl Guides of Canada, and anything else you can get your hands on. You work hard with children who have special needs, without ever complaining, teaching them to learn and love themselves. You never spend money on yourself. You never buy the expensive shoes or the newest jacket. Your money always goes towards groceries, pizza days, school supplies, and university applications. Your free time is spent taking us to doctors and to recitals or sports practices, instead of using the time to pamper yourself.

You're always there to give your opinion, believing in honesty and good judgement. From your naval ring to your tattoo, you're a prime example of how some people never get old. From the moment I saw you and the first time you held me in your arms you were, and always will be, my mom and my hero.

Kierra Emond-Galan, 17

Brenda Brooks

My mom has sacrificed her whole life for me. When I was born, she quit her job so she could raise me up right through my childhood. She gave me the love in her heart and the support for me to do well. Even though we did not have very much money, it never affected me. All I remember are the good times we had together.

When I was very depressed at one point in my life, my mom was there. Nothing seemed to be going my way. All my luck had seemed to have gone down the drain. I felt that I had failed in life, by the age of 11. I had let down my teachers, my friends, and myself. Most of all, I felt that I had let down my parents. I found myself crying in my room with the door shut. My mom quietly came in my room and sat beside me. She talked about what was good in my life, what I had accomplished and, most of all, she told me how proud she was of me. We sat together for almost an hour until my emotional wounds were healed.

That day, she told me about her struggles in life and how she had conquered them. She also told me that somewhere in the world, someone had it worse than I did. It didn't mean too much at the time, but whenever I am down, I always remember that someone in the world has it worse and I begin to think about what I have done in my life. It instantly makes me feel uplifted and happy. It really makes me appreciate my mom and what she does for me.

Solomon Mason, 14

Barb Drenth

My mom and I have been through a lot. We've moved seven times, but now we are in a nice place to stay for awhile. My mom does great stuff for me and sometimes I don't appreciate it. So I want to say thanks, mom. Thanks for keeping me in your dreams.

Thanks for not getting an abortion when you were 18 and pregnant with me, even though some people wanted you to. Thanks for teaching me how to walk and how to talk and mostly, thanks for teaching me how to stand up for myself. Thank you for all of my talents, like being able to sing, dance and act. Thank you also for putting me in all of my activities, like cheerleading and soccer. I'd especially like to thank you for helping out with the new house.

Also, I want to say thanks for my nana and papa. Without them, I wouldn't be in half of the things that I am in today and I also wouldn't have most of the nice things I have today. Without all of these people in my life I wouldn't be able to live my life the way I like. I really love all these people, but my mom means the most to me. I love you, mom, and that's never going to change!

Kayleigh Drenth, 13

Nancy Armstrong

My hero has inspired me in
Ways I can't explain.
My hero can't jump over
buildings
And she doesn't wear a cape.
My hero is loving and caring
And brave in her own way.
My hero is my mother in
These ways and much more,
I thank her and appreciate
Her always being there.

Lisa Walker, 14

Liz Brooks

Since I was little, as far back as I can remember, my mother has always been there for me. She's helped me with all of my problems. I've gone through depression and my mama is the one who I can say helped me the most. She was there when no one else could deal with my mood swings. She was there for me when my cousin committed suicide and when my dog was put down. She helps with all the regularities of everyday life. Now most people think that that's a parent's job - to look after their kids, to do everything for their child. But there is only so much that is mandatory and the rest is out of pure love.

In the past year, my sister checked into rehab for multiple addictions. I was upset for many reasons, some still unknown. I was scared to face her by myself. I was afraid to be brought to reality. My mama encouraged me to say what I needed to say, so that I could resolve my problems.

My parents took my sister's children into our home. It was the right choice, I know, but it doesn't make it any easier to deal with. Many things changed. My parents had less time for me because the kids needed more attention. They can't take care of themselves like I can. My mama has still managed to help me, but not as much as before. My mother has done everything for these kids, from washing their clothes and cooking their meals to supervising on class trips and getting involved in extra-curricular activities.

She takes me to appointments and friends' houses. When I ask for help, she'll stop what she's doing to help me because she puts everyone else before herself and her issues. She rarely does anything for herself and if she does, it usually involves helping other people, too. My grandpa has Alzheimer's disease and that is someone else that she takes care of. My mama always has and always will care for my gram's health and assets.

My mama has saved me time and time again from multiple obstacles but, at the same time, has known when to step back. I can honestly say that from my mother, I have learned how to help others, which in turn will help me. You mean the world to me, Mama, just as you tell me I mean the world to you.

Kiersten Brooks, 16

CHAPTER FOUR

OUR DADS

Any man can be a father, but it takes a special person to be a dad.

Proverb

Dean McCubbin
(Keeper of the Grail)

It starts simply with recognizing that your dad isn't going to be around forever. It's another one of those ideas you've always known and yet chosen to ignore until it seemed dangerous to do so. Suffice it to say, knowing doesn't make it any easier.

Where do you begin with a man who not only has touched your life, but the lives of so many others around you. I spoke once with a friend about my father and he said, "When he's gone, the world will be a sadder place for all those who never had a chance to meet him".

I once laughed at how many people my dad knew. No matter where we traveled, he always found someone in town to wave to and as he used to say, 'chew the fat' with. I cannot count the number of times I've been introduced to people he knew and that he believed I should get to know. I'm sure somewhere along the line I should have done more networking. To those of you reading this, I'm Dean McCubbin's son. Remember me.

I don't ever want to forget what I learned from my father. I'm aiming to repeat the beauty of his life with my wife and two children. It is a great struggle because I don't have his faith or his serenity to accept the things I cannot change. Where I have little sayings that I find intriguing and life-affirming, he had words by which he lived. My motivations for living, written on slips of paper, or tucked into poetry books, are merely a shadow of the witticisms and philosophies of life that lay under the faded glass blotter atop his desk. I would sit at that desk and read those words of wisdom and pretend to be my father, sharpening red Canadore College pencils, of which there seemed to be thousands, and tapping them on the eraser end, like I was Johnny Carson. I would wear an orange-coloured rubber thimble and expertly flip through his papers, making sure to leave them just as I had found them. I would attempt to use the rustic, black and gold letter opener and imagine myself receiving important documents in the mail. What I remember the most, though, is the desk lamp. You had to hold the red button down long enough to get the fluorescent tube to light up and this was no mere feat. I remember, as a kid, trying to get it to stop flickering. This required precision timing. To control dad's lamp with this type of dexterity was, for me, a rite of passage. I've been trying to shine like him ever since.

My father taught me to light a candle and not curse the darkness. I think often of this credo when I lack the energy to start a fire with which I can see the path more clearly. He always said, "God Be With You" before I went to bed as a child, and I recognize now how lucky I was to have somebody, 'anybody' watching out for me. He told me 70% of the things we worry about never come to pass and, no matter how unlucky you feel sometimes, there's always someone out there far worse off than you.

My father's generosity was always obvious to me and I'm sure his random acts of kindness were inspired by his mother and father who, during the depression, gave to the hobos who rode the rails. His family lived by the railroad tracks, so it would have been impossible not to observe the downtrodden. This outpouring to the needy permeated my life and I recall countless times climbing over family members to make my way to the edge of the church pew, where dad was waiting with the collection basket to accept the envelope. He could have put it in himself at the back of the church, but I think he did it this way to remind me of what it means to give to others. Dad and Mom always made sure I had my orange and black UNICEF box carefully tied around my neck before I went out for Halloween. They figured I was getting candy, so I'd better be paying for it in some way, by never being allowed to forget that other children didn't have any food to eat, much less candy. At any rate, his mother and father showed him and he, in turn, showed me that you must give even when you have little, for your reward will be great.

My father is a treasure and even though he has not rescued anyone from a burning building or carried a wounded soldier from no man's land back to safety, he is my hero. I cannot think of anyone who has known him to ever say an unkind word about him. He has been an asset to his community, a shining example of his faith, and a precious gift to his large and happy family. I have been truly blessed to grow up in his extravagant shadow. The world is a better place because of him. And I am a better man.

Rob McCubbin

Peter Ricketts

My daddy is special. He loves me a lot by talking to me when I need him. He spends time playing with me and we go shopping together. He makes me laugh a lot.

My daddy is always there when I need to talk to him about important stuff, like if something is wrong at school. He tells me about animals.

We go to the mall for ice cream. We go to the bookstore. We go to the movie theatre. We love to eat popcorn and licorice and chocolate.

He makes me laugh when he tickles me. He makes me laugh when he tells jokes.

My daddy is the best daddy on earth!

Danielle Ricketts, 9

Dave McClatchie
(The Wind beneath my Wings)

My father has played many roles in my life…a parent, an advisor, a teacher, a sounding board, and a leader. I have watched him lead our family, my high school, and my home community. I have admired him as a man, a husband, a father, and a grandfather. He has influenced many people in many different ways. He has taught me many valuable lessons, some through his strength, and others through his tears. It is these lessons that I am often most thankful for. It is his humanity that makes him my hero.

Tears send an incredible message and make an indelible mark on our lives. Many of the lessons that I have learned throughout my life have often been precipitated by them. My father taught me these lessons and punctuated them with the tears I once believed he never shed.

On a warm spring day in the early 80's, our beautiful golden retriever, Lady, died. She was dad's pride and joy - loyal and kind, like him. Mom drove the truck 45 minutes to the nearest animal hospital that day, with dad in the back, cradling her body with his. My brother and I were in the front with mom, watching helplessly. I saw dad cry for the first time that day. That day, I learned to value the life of all of God's creatures, as much as my own. I also learned the price of loyalty and compassion, and that Dad was human.

Not so many years went by, when I took a very sick and struggling cat to the vet. Ginger and I had spent a loving 16 years together. With her life hanging in the balance, the vet called my family at home to speak to my parents about the tough decision that needed to be made. With me listening in on the line, the decision was made to let Ginger go. I cried and I was angry, but I found the strength that day to do what needed to be done. When I got home from the vet's office, my father greeted me at the door. He held me close and cried with me. On that day, my father's tears taught me that parenting is an ominous responsibility and you cannot protect your children from the perils of life, but you can weather the storm alongside them.

When I married, I found a man that could be my hero in a very different way and I love him for that. But I am not a sentimental woman and I can honestly say that I remember only a few interesting stories from my wedding day. My father-daughter dance would be one. I can remember the feeling of being held so tight, I couldn't breathe. I can remember the love and the tears. I can remember the crowd watching us dance, but what I remember the most about that moment in time, is the song that played...Dad, "Did you ever know that you're my hero?"

It has now been almost three years since my father was diagnosed with cancer. He called me himself to tell me the news. It knocked the wind out of me. I was stunned and sad and confused. Like millions of people before me, I looked to the heavens and asked, "Why?" But, like all the times we'd cried together in the past, there were lessons to be learned through this. I was reminded that...

· Families grow stronger with every challenge that they face together.

- There is no time like the present to tell a loved one just how much they are loved.
- Now is also a good time to forgive and forget family flaws.
- Tomorrow is another day, new challenges, and new pieces of life to live.
- Children can handle anything with the right training and a loving family by their side, and
- Every child needs a hero.

Dad, you are, and always have been, "The Wind beneath my Wings..."

Michelle Graham

Dick Wyga

My dad is one of my heroes. Not for any special reason, just because he's my dad. He did the things that the dads of his generation did. He worked through the week, did yard and house duty on Saturdays, and went to church and relaxed with his family on Sundays. Nothing special, really, but he's my dad.

He taught me many things. Of course, many of these lessons were not absorbed until I became a parent, myself. Dad taught me about sacrifice and devotion to family. How many times we children smirked around the supper table when Dad would doze off after eating, while the Bible was being read. After I became a mother of four small boys, I fell into the same trap of the after-supper lull (just as the boys got their umpteenth burst of energy while I, having finally sat still for a few moments to eat, now felt a bed and blanket would be the perfect dessert). I then came to appreciate how tired Dad, the plasterer, must have been after working a long and physically active day. But that's what dads did - they worked hard and supported their families.

Dad taught me how to care for and improve the house you lived in and make it a home. When I was six years old, Dad decided to buy a 100-acre farm with no plumbing, little electricity, and a very decrepit house. An adventure for me and my five older siblings, but many hours of sweat went into transforming that farmhouse into a home to be proud of. Again, not until I had a place of my own did I look back and marvel at all the work both Mom and Dad put into the home of my youth. But that's what dads did - they took care of their homes and families.

My dad taught me how to spend family time together. Camping week in tents, random car trips with no destination in mind, and many walks through the bush on the farm property are just some of my happiest childhood memories. How idyllic they seem to me now! Why were the family trips with my own children so much preparation, so chaotic and noisy, so exhausting? My dad had six kids to contend with. My husband and I had only four! But that's what dads did - they spent quality time with their families.

Dad taught me about God and the place we have in this world, as well as the next. And it wasn't so much in the way we would think of today, but in the way of his generation, by attending church, reading the Bible, and praying on a regular basis. As an adult, I began to see my dad in a different light - how his steadfastness, solidity, and dependability made a great impact on his family. As a teenager, I discovered that my dad prayed for us, his children, every night. And as the family grew with the in-laws and grandchildren, they were added to his prayers. And when the great-grandchildren joined the list, well, is it any coincidence that Dad began taking naps around that time? And as life went on with its ups and downs, its tragedies and blessings, it became a comfort to know that Dad was always praying for us, his children. But that's what dads did - they loved their families.

Dad is gone now. But the lessons he taught me will be with me forever and if I can share even a fragment of what he taught me with my children, they will be blessed.

Sandy Biffis-Kri

Gerald Humphrey

Every child believes that their parents will never go away and up until the day of his passing I, at the age of 25, still believed that to be true. My dad, Gerald Humphrey, was the most unforgettable person you could ever meet. His bubbling personality and his striking resemblance to Mr. Miagi was definitely hard to forget. He had a smile that would brighten anyone's day. He was always there when he was needed and was a man whom you would always want on your side. He never had any enemies.

Dad had suffered from cardiomyopathy, a disease of the heart, since I was 13 years old. I never heard him complain, nor did it stop him from doing what he enjoyed. Playing with his eight grandchildren was always on the top of his priority list. I will always remember him saying, "I may look okay on the outside, but on the inside, I'm falling apart". As a young kid, I didn't really understand but, as I grew older, I started to realize what he meant. But he would mask the pain. You wouldn't know what his body was going through on the inside, from how he looked and acted on the outside.

His family and his friends always came first. He would never put himself before others and was a man of his word. I was 16 months old when I was adopted and I will never forget Dad telling me that, when he first saw my picture, he said, "I finally found my little girl". No matter how old I get, that will never change. Dad was a wonderful husband, father, and friend. He was loved by many. He was a machinist up until he was forced into early retirement due to his condition, but not a day went by that he didn't keep busy.

If there is one thing that my dad taught his children, it was that God works in mysterious ways and you never know when your time is up. Life is too short to sweat the small stuff and you must live each day as if it were your last. Nothing meant more to him than the happiness and health of his family.

Shannon Humphrey Cusmanic

Barry Austin

If I had to choose one person who I look up to the most, I would choose my father, Barry Austin. My dad has taught me many things, both practical and abstract. For many years, my father, like his father, Kirby, worked as a carpenter. Many houses and cottages in the Muskoka area were built by my dad and grandfather. As the prices for custom-built houses increased and the demand decreased, Barry and Kirby were forced to move on to other work. For a short time, my dad taught college courses on woodworking. Ever since I was young, he has taught me how to build and how to renovate. Projects we have helped each other complete include building decks, a basketball net, speaker boxes, shelves, cabinets, and tree houses. My dad sometimes takes me on small renovation jobs and has hired my help for a weekend or two.

As a young man, my dad went to college for electronics and owned a motorcycle. He learned much about basic electronics and mechanics. If I ever have a problem and need to fix or build something, my dad always has an idea how to help and has the resources to do it. Our basement is filled with tools of all kinds. He owns a table saw, a drill press, and about a dozen toolboxes full of tools. If that isn't enough to take up our limited basement real estate, the model train layout takes up the rest.

My dad has a strong interest in trains and model railroading. For many years, he was a respected member of the recently-disbanded North Bay Model Railroad Club. Dad knows many interesting facts about trains and where to find them. Just last summer, my dad and I went on a trip to Cobalt to see different sights and train stations. When I was very young, he helped me start my own collection of model trains and has shown me how to build, paint, and maintain them.

When my dad was younger, he listened to classic rock such as Led Zeppelin, The Guess Who, and so on. I have similar interests in music and we often talk about classic rock. He will always have something new to suggest that I listen to and always asks if I know the song playing on the radio. I have learned much about music from him and I'm glad we can share the same taste in music. Every summer evening, my dad and I eat supper outside in our backyard. It's nice to sit out and listen to music and talk. We often find ourselves talking about politics, science, and world issues. This is another way I've found that I have learned much from my father.

Since my dad has only just recently begun to learn about computers and technology, and since I love computers, I give back to him by helping him with all of his technological problems. I only wish I could carry on the family profession of being a carpenter, but the age in which we now live revolves more and more around technology. My dad always has something interesting to say and I always like having him around. We get along very well and learn from each other every day.

Mike Austin, 17

Robert Dampier

My dad, Robert, always strives to do better. No matter what it is, he always sets his goals higher. A lot of people will pick professional athletes as their hero, but none of them could make as much of a difference in my life as my dad. No matter what, he never settles for anything but first.

There are many obstacles that my dad has had to overcome to get to where he is today. I remember many nights when he stayed up reading and studying so he could get what he wanted. He spent the day with his family, or at work, and spent his nights with the books. When he finally wrote and passed the tests, I had never felt such joy, such pride in anyone, knowing that the hard work and sleepless nights had paid off. He now works for the government, maintaining computers and networks.

All of who my dad is, and what he has done to get to where he is, is an inspiration to me. He is the reason I'm in school and working hard to get what I want. He's the reason I strive to be better every day and why I reach above and always try to do better. He showed me that anything is possible if you work for it. Dreams can be a reality if you want them to be. Be strong and always believe.

Craig Dampier

Sam Hodgson

Sam Hodgson is a double amputee who lost his legs in 1981, at the age of 39. He was a very fit and active man and many people wondered how this was going to affect Sam and his spirit. I never doubted his fighting spirit.

Sam went on to compete in the Special Olympics, in the early 1980's, in three disciplines: javelin, shot-put, and discus. He came home with medals in all three events. Sam returned to school to get a diploma in computer programming and worked in that field for 25 years. He never missed work, even on the days when he had to shovel his driveway.

Sam has a camp where he loves to spend time, just fishing and kayaking. He takes care of all the maintenance himself. Sam continues to be in great physical health at the age of 65, working out regularly at the military base. Several people tell me that on some days, when they don't feel like exercising, they think of Sam and then get moving.

Sam is currently helping two friends build their third airplane together and is excited every day to get up and face life and its challenges. He always has a smile on his face and touches everyone he comes in contact with. Sam is not only my dad, he's a great role model!

Deborah Reid

Rob Witiuk

It was just a regular Saturday when my dad went to work at about 4:00 in the morning. Like every other overtime shift, he didn't even have to be there. He worked at the Goodyear OTR plant, where he made tires. My dad was a workaholic. He loved his job, even though some people didn't appreciate all the work he did.

While my dad was at work, my grandma and I were sleeping and my mom had gone to Tim Horton's to get her coffee. While my mom was out, the phone rang and someone left a message on our answering machine. Since it was so early in the morning, my mom didn't think to check for messages. About a half an hour later, the phone rang again and it was one of my dad's co-workers, saying that my dad had been in a serious accident. My mom had only four words to say to that, "I'm on my way". At this point on my mom panicked, as she feared what might happen and what she'd be faced with.

I woke up at around 8:00 a.m., and I came in to see my grandma (the one that doesn't live with us) sitting in the living room. For some strange reason, I knew something was wrong, because why would my mom not be there when I woke up? I was in grade 8 at the time, so I was smart enough to figure it out. My grandma was the one who told me, but I didn't really know what to think. I didn't cry at first because I wasn't exactly sure of the situation, but when it hit me, I cried for about two days. Not knowing was definitely the worst part of it.

My mom arrived at his workplace and she was told that, while my dad was working inside the tire, he felt the tire stand jerk a bit. Naturally, he got out of the tire and went to check to see if there was a problem. Unfortunately, there was. The stand collapsed on him and over 2,000 pounds of rubber came down on him, crushing his pelvis and damaging his bladder.

My mom immediately went to the hospital after she saw my dad being taken on a stretcher to the ambulance. My parents' best friends and my grandpa went to the hospital as well. Dad had to be air-lifted to Sunnybrook Hospital in Toronto right away because his condition was very serious. After my dad was air-lifted, my mom came home to pack her clothes and head down so she would be there for him when he got out of surgery. While my mom was home for that short period of time, she told me roughly some of the details of what was going on. I just cried. My mom had to leave and all I was able to do was sit at home, not knowing what was happening. Whether my dad was going to live or die wasn't clear to anyone.

About two weeks after the accident, I was finally able to go visit my dad. It was probably one of the hardest things ever, to see him in the condition he was in: tubes everywhere, yellow, and about 100 pounds heavier than before because of all the swelling and fluid buildup inside him.

After being in Sunnybrook for one week short of a month, my dad was well enough to be transferred to the North Bay hospital. Along with him came plates, screws, and pins holding him together. One month stuck in the hospital wasn't exactly paradise but after that my dad was able to live at home again and, thankfully, be home for Christmas.

Challenges and obstacles never really stopped my dad from getting to where he needed to be, even if that meant learning to walk again. Determined but frustrated, he slowly regained his ability to walk, even when doctors thought he wouldn't walk again. My dad proved them and everyone else wrong!

Thinking about my dad and how life panned out for us, I'm extremely thankful for what I have because no one can really know what they've got until it's gone, or until it's put in jeopardy. I've learned that bad things happen to innocent people and that anyone who has strength and faith can get through anything, whether it's they, themselves, who have faith or their friends and family who help them. To show the faith and strength my family had at the time and continues to have, each member of my family got matching tattoos, meaning "faith", on our ankles. The faith symbol is there to remind us that, no matter what happens, you've got to have faith.

It seems like yesterday that the accident happened. It's something that will never leave us. I'm so proud of my mom for being strong, not only for herself, but for everyone else, especially me. I'm most proud of my dad for never wanting to quit and being the strong man that he is. I've never told my dad, but he is my hero and I can say that I feel privileged to have him in my life.

Lindsay Witiuk, 16

Brian Stephens

Brian Stephens has raised me on his own, with the help of my grandparents, for the past 18 years. Here is a poem explaining how important he is to me.

The First Man I Met

Memories of laughs and giggles
He makes my heart shine
Dries my tears when I cry
He stands behind me in all
Picks me up when I fall
He must wear a bullet proof vest,
'Cause he always stands up to the test
He's got a heart of gold
That cannot be sold
Sleepless nights and bedtime stories
He was there for it all
If troubled, he's the first one I'd call
Our times spent together I wouldn't trade
He's special. It's just the way he was made
His parents were Irish, he's a wonderful lad
He's my saviour, my hero, my best friend
He's my dad

Jessica Stephens, 18

CHAPTER FIVE

OUR GONE BUT NOT FORGOTTEN HEROES

Death ends a life, not a relationship.

Jack Lemmon

Jacky Vander Valk
("I Love You Too . . .")

I passed away last Sunday. I was only 34. It's too young to die, in my opinion, but in this case my opinion doesn't count.

I'd been sick for eight years. I was completely healthy at age 26 - or so I thought. Then one day without notice, I felt something wasn't normal. I felt different. The doctor said the difference that I was feeling was M.S. - Multiple Sclerosis.

No way. Not me. My career is going awesome. I have Jacky, my amazing wife. We just had a beautiful little girl, Tia. Life is great. How can I have M.S.?

I did. I had M.S. Me. I still don't believe it.

I know it's been hard on Jacky and Tia. It's been hard on our whole family. One of the things that have made me happy throughout this whole, eight-year ordeal is my friends and family. I have overheard them saying that my attitude has been amazing the whole time. I suffered in silence a lot. I tried not to cry until after my friends and family were long gone after their visits. I wanted to be strong in front of them.

Even when they came to see me, I managed to give them the thumbs-up sign to let them know I was doing okay. I am pretty sure they saw me smile through my oxygen mask, too. It's the legacy I want to leave my family: no matter what - you can have a great attitude. Jacky has suffered as much as me. She has to raise Tia without me. The bright side, for Jacky, is she gets to see her everyday. I'll do what I can to help my wife, my hero, from here.

Jacky is my hero for many reasons; my hero, right up to the end and beyond. A couple of days before I passed, Tia was making a heart picture that she wanted to give to me. It said, "I love you Daddy, Love Tia." Unfortunately, I "graduated" before Tia could get her artwork to me. "Oh no, Mommy, how will Daddy get his picture now?" said our sad little angel. Jacky hesitated, collected her thoughts, and bravely fought back her tears before she replied, "Don't worry, sweetheart, we'll make sure the picture gets to Daddy in heaven."

As well as going through all of the funeral preparations, I knew Jacky would figure out a way to keep her promise. Sure enough, after the funeral, the family made their way to the gravesite. "Look, Mommy, Daddy got my note!" shrieked our happy little girl. At the very bottom of the tombstone (in small, but distinct letters) Tia saw these words engraved: "I love you too Tia."

Rob Vander Valk
Shared through Barry Spilchuk and Paul Barton

Editor's Note: Here are small excerpts from the poem that Jacky Vander Valk wrote about her husband and read at his funeral.

I'll do it, I said, as I pretend to be strong,
This isn't fair, please, let them be wrong.
I'll do it, I said, as I steadied his hand
I try not to think of all we had planned.

I'll do it, I said, as I sold our dream home
It's difficult now to sleep alone.
He did it, I said, as I remember his life
I must say goodbye. I loved you dearly, your wife.

Bryan Sargent
(From Hero to Zero and Back Again)

My dad, Bryan Sargent, could do everything in my eyes, even save the world. He's an amazing person. He taught half the city and was known for his inspirational coaching.

He was in better shape than everyone in my class when he was 58. Every day he exercised and, in the summer, he ran at least six kilometres every day. I never thought my dad was old for he never acted his age. My dad was the one who took my interest in sports seriously and was my personal coach who always had a pep talk to make me better, the best. He was the greatest coach I ever had because he was there at every game and took time out of his day to help me with my skill work. He taught me all the basics. Other coaches have helped me develop as well but, at the end of the day, my dad was still my number one coach.

My dad was one of the only people I wanted to talk to. Every discussion I had with him, I learned something new. I would always ask him questions about school work or some plays in sports because he always knew how to explain things so that I actually understood. Dad was like my library. If I needed some help, I went straight to him. He was always willing to share.

I've always wanted to be like my dad. He knew everything, was in excellent shape, could fix every problem, and was known by everyone. Every day, I tried to be like him. I pushed myself when we were running so that I could run just as far as he and I would try to remember everything he told me. I tried fixing some problems but, in the end, dad had to come and unfix what I had done. I wanted to grow up to be an amazing coach and teacher and still be able to keep up with my children even though I was old. But as I grew up and learned from, and talked to, dad, I realized that I had to become my own person and that I couldn't be exactly like dad. All I know is that no matter what I choose to be in the future, I can only wish to be as amazing a person and parent as Bryan Sargent.

However, on Victoria Day last year, my hero disappeared. My dad became very sick and, in the blink of an eye, my life changed. My dad was in the hospital for a month, the longest he's ever been away from me and my family. It felt so surreal to not have him around. When my dad finally came home, he was very weak and looked like he had aged 10 years. He could barely walk down the street and had no mood for those long conversations we used to have. This new dad scared me and sometimes I avoided him. I just couldn't stand to look at what used to be the most amazing man ever, my hero.

At the beginning of summer, he had to go to Sudbury for some testing. When mom and dad came back, mom was crying. My mom never cried, but I guess I had to get used to it because my dad's condition went from horrible to unfathomable. My dad sat there, very calmly looking at us, and said, "Things are going to change around here. We went up to Sudbury to get some test results and they showed that I have cancer in my bowel..." He went on to say more, but I wouldn't listen. I just couldn't stop crying. They say that, one day, your hero will fall and mine just did.

Going from being a normal family to having someone diagnosed with cancer is horrible, but for it to be my dad was the end of my world. When I was little, I was listening to my dad on the phone late at night. I was thinking and thinking and I can't remember how I came along this train of thought, but all I can remember was looking up at my ceiling and, out of nowhere, thinking 'the worst thing that could ever happen to my dad would be for him to get cancer.' I cried for hours over that thought and he was still healthy. I had no idea what cancer was, except that my aunt had died from it and that it was incurable. Now, I'm 15 and I know way too much about it.

It's been almost a year that my dad has had cancer and we've had our highs and lows. Life isn't fair; I've learned that the hard way. I'm now beginning to accept that my dad has cancer and that he can't do what he used to do. At the beginning of all of this, it had seemed as though my hero was gone forever. He had only changed and that's life. My dad has gone through unimaginable pain and has survived so much when it would have been easy for him to throw in the towel. He promised us that he would fight for as long as he could and my dad is not one to lie. He has developed into the most amazing person ever who lost almost everything he had and yet he still fights. I try talking to him now and sometimes I get him in a good mood. I help him as much as I can because I took my father for granted once; it's not going to happen again.

He was always there for me and now it's my turn to be there for him. Daddy, I love you so much. We all do. Please get better!

Katie Sargent, 15

Editor's Note: Bryan Sargent lost his battle with cancer on August 10, 2007. Our thoughts and prayers go out to Bryan's family as they mourn the loss of their hero.

Bernie Donovan

I was 10 months old when my biological father left to serve in World War Two, along with most of my older, male relatives. I was 23 when we were re-united. In the meantime, my parents divorced. When my mother was 22, she had to work in Ottawa to support both of us, so I was sent to live on my grandparents' isolated farm outside Avonmore, in eastern Ontario. I was a three-year-old girl and an only child. At a very young age, I had no choice but to become independent and entertain myself while living with significantly older (I thought) and wonderful grandparents. For the next five years, barnyard animals were my friends and associates and, yes, I walked a mile every day to a little red school house, usually despite the weather.

As an only child, the fact that I didn't have a father like the other kids in my class or like my large family of cousins made me feel like an outsider when families got together. In the meantime, my godfather, Bernie Donovan, came back to Canada on a hospital ship, with a collapsed lung, and spent months recuperating.

Bernie fell in love with my mother, Thelma, in the years that followed. They married when I was eight and we went to live in Arnprior, Ontario, where this new man in our lives was a constable with the O.P.P. He loved cowboy movies, could dance a jig, and loved to joke. He was also tall, dark, handsome, very young-looking, and he had eyes only for my mother.

One day, a lawyer from Ottawa came to visit and I recall being asked if I wanted Bernie to be my new father and also to change my last name. What fatherless child would turn that deal down? Suddenly, I had a new last name and a daddy like all the other kids in my new school. We were a normal family. The only drawback was that I was now a cop's daughter and was expected to set an example for other kids. That didn't work. But from the day he legally adopted me, Bernie Donovan always thought of me and treated me as his very own flesh and blood. Very few knew the truth.

My only nemesis was a girl named Maryellen who, for whatever reason, needed the daily exercise of pounding me to a pulp! She wasn't much bigger than I was, hiding behind trees and ready to pounce; that is, until my new father took me into the back yard and taught me how to defend myself. After that, Maryellen and I became really good friends! And if I admired my mother for her many talents, daddy had become my hero.

I remember bringing home a puppy, saying 'someday' had arrived. My mother named the dog 'Lucky' because she said the dog would be lucky to live there. My father, a dog- and horse-lover at heart, spent an afternoon building a gate across the kitchen door, to keep the dog out of the living room. The ordinary gate would have served its purpose had my father adhered to the original plan. But the plan didn't work, much to my mother's distress, after he spent that same evening teaching the dog how to jump the gate. Lucky loved all the neighbourhood kids. He followed all of us to school until, one day, an ice-cream truck driver had to make the choice between hitting two kids and hitting our dog. As Lucky lay in agony on the street, my father, tears in his eyes, had to use his police revolver and shot his own dog. He never forgot that.

He showed me that revolver once; it hung on the back of his bedroom door. He took it apart, explained to me how it worked, how it was loaded, and then he hung it back up in the holster with the warning never to touch it. I never did. He had taught me how to defend myself. He painted a second-hand bike and taught me how to ride it. He also taught me to fish, fire a rifle, ride a horse, and play baseball; there was money for roller skates, figure skates, and music lessons. He later joined the Royal Canadian Air Force and worked in Special Investigations. Even then, when I needed a shoulder to cry on, it was his. And I vowed he would be my daddy until the day he died.

For 50 years, this man adored my mother and when she died of cancer 10 years ago in London, Ontario, he was devastated! He was also in the middle stages of Alzheimers. There was only one solution in my book. It was simply my turn to be the caregiver. I packed up all of his personal belongings in my car and we came to his new home. At first, while I was working, I took him to adult daycare, until a nursing-home bed became available. On the weekends, he was ours to spoil!

My adult children and my daughter-in-law were wonderful with him and he adored his three great-grandchildren, who called him, "G.G. Pa". Was it difficult to watch his mind silently and gradually diminish? At times, yes; but otherwise, not really. This once-handsome man, and the smoothest dance partner I've ever had, was withering away to a shell, so I hid his photos. The blessing was that he was unaware that, in a very short time, he had lost his wife, his car, his home and furniture, his friends, and his ability to play his favorite sport, golf. If he couldn't remember, then I stubbornly refused to. If he had to live in the present, then so would I! I lived in his present each and every time I visited him. When he mumbled something I couldn't understand, I replied, "Oh, I didn't know that" or, "Who told you?" or words to that effect. It satisfied him. I hired an alternate care-giver to take him for walks and drives while I was working, so he could still see the world around him. How could we not afford him the same love, patience, acceptance, and kindness he had given freely to us?

I remember leaving the nursing home one afternoon with tears rolling down my cheeks. I looked skyward and said out loud, "You can take him now," for I knew my father wouldn't have wanted to live that way anymore. As I started to drive away, I suddenly smiled to myself, imagining that perhaps there was a much more authoritative voice than mine coming from above, replying, "Excuse Me! That's MY choice, not yours!"

And so it was. His only child and his three grandchildren were with him when he died peacefully, a year later. But it was a "good grief" and he will, forever, be my daddy.

Judy Donovan-McDonald

Barbara Saunders
(The Cycle of Life)

The story I really want to focus on is about my sister-in-law, Barbara. She and her brother, Gordon, were 13 years apart. They were wonderful friends, loved each other, and enjoyed each other's company very much. We became very close over the years, always getting together for family functions and going on trips together, along with Barbara's husband, Mark. We spent a lot of time on the phone catching up on day-to-day news. She always had a story to tell!

Barbara was a huge Blue Jays fan, so we often traveled to Toronto together for ball games. Barbara and Mark had two children, Nancy and Matthew. We had many family gatherings; any excuse to get together for cake. Barbara would have a cake for the kids on the first day of school, the last day of school, birthdays, the anniversary of anything, Easter, Halloween, religious celebrations, graduations, you name it; we called her the 'queen of cakes'!

In the fall of 2002, just after Mark retired from the Fire Department, Barbara was diagnosed with stage-four ovarian cancer. We were stunned that this beautiful woman, who lived her life to please her family, friends, students, and church, and tried to be kind and do nothing but good things, could be faced with this horrible disease. At a time when we were devastated with this news, Barbara faced it head-on, going into chemotherapy treatments with such a positive attitude. She thought of nothing but getting the cancer into remission and the two-to-five-years that the doctors said were possible with remission. You see, she had a lot to live for. Her daughter and her husband had just announced they were expecting their first baby, and Barbara's first grandchild, in September. Barbara wanted so much to be a grandmother and she was determined to be there for the birth of that baby!

As the fall turned into winter, there were many complications with the treatments, along with a lengthy hospital stay, surgery and follow up during SARS, hair loss, and sickness. Barbara never said, "Why me?" She made it very easy for us. Barbara was very strong in her faith and that was a big comfort to her at a difficult time. As she progressed with her treatments, there was a brief interval when she was feeling better. But during this time I, too, started to have some health problems and was diagnosed with stage-one ovarian cancer! They say this is a rare disease; only two percent of women will get it in their lifetime and we both had the same disease at the same time. I also had to have surgery and chemotherapy. My wonderful sister-in-law called me every time I went for my treatments, to see how I was. Even though I was much better than she, she was so concerned about me. She sent food over after my surgery and wanted to be there for me.

Spring came and I was still in active treatment. Barbara's chemotherapy was not working. She was not beating the disease as much as she fought it. Nancy was getting bigger and planning for the birth of the baby, due in September, and Barbara was planning to be there for her. Over the summer, she became weaker and was hospitalized in August. She called us all up to the hospital and had ordered a cake to celebrate Kennedy, the unborn baby. It was unbelievable. Here we were, celebrating the miracle of a new life and the end of another but, again, Barbara made it easy for us all. I was still going through chemotherapy and would go to the hospital every day to spend as much time with her as I could, and to give Mark a break. She always asked how I was and wanted to just sit and talk. She loved to have company and welcomed any visitor that came to see her. Mark was there almost every moment. She was everything to him.

On September 9th, Kennedy was born! Barbara's son-in-law, Jody, made arrangements to bring the baby over to see her the next day, escorted by a nurse from the nursery. Barbara got to visit with, and hold, her granddaughter over the next two days. She grew increasingly weaker and asked to see us all. As I sat beside her bed and held her hand, she thanked me for being such a wonderful sister-in-law and said she was sorry she wouldn't be able to be there for me if I needed her. I couldn't even speak. It was the most difficult day of my life - to say goodbye to this wonderful lady who brought only love and joy to everyone's life and who wasn't going to be with us any longer. It just wasn't fair. On September 13, 2003, surrounded by all her family, Barbara lost her battle.

We have all moved on with our lives. I have been cancer-free for four years now. One of the most difficult, but delightful, times is when I see Kennedy. She is an amazing little girl. She is soon to be four years old and so much like her grandmother; full of spunk and always ready for an adventure. It is such a reminder, when I see her, that Barbara is not here and missing out on so much. I know you are with us, Barbara. Not a day goes by that I don't miss you and think of you. I miss our chats. Your loving sister-in-law,

Lynda Smith

Kathy Sirrs

Kathy was, without a doubt, the most glamorous warrior. In the first few years, when she was still working, she would quite often arrive fashionably late for practice. I say 'fashionably' because she'd be wearing her business clothes, make up, and great hair. She'd come running down to the lake, her paddle and lifejacket in hand, flashing that smile. After a quick change into her paddling clothes, she'd be ready to go. Even her paddling clothes were snappy. How many paddlers have shoulder pads in their racing shirts?!!

She was an exceptional public speaker and soon became a very visible spokesperson for our team. She was so passionate about our mission of raising awareness about breast cancer and certainly was an inspiration for many. I would say that Kathy was our media darling. She was very comfortable in that role and it gave her the opportunity to express her feelings about the disease and impress upon those who listened to her, how very important it was for everyone to do what they could to help eradicate all the suffering that goes along with it.

I didn't really get to know Kathy until our 2005 paddling season. She sat behind me on the bus when we went to our out-of-town festivals. I discovered her amazing sense of humour and her refreshing honesty in our conversations about life. I learned of her fears about her health and how very deeply she cared for her family and how she worried about their future without her. Listening to her, I realized that for Kathy, each day was an ongoing battle. It was so easy to forget this as she had such courage and vitality.

At festivals in 2005 and 2006, she taught me how to sweet-talk the vendors into lowering the price of an item and she had me in stitches, watching her flirt with the young, muscular, male paddlers! She confessed to me, "You know, I can be a real flirt. I hope I never stop!" and then she would flash me one of those smiles. She was fun!

Last September, Kathy and I participated in the Weekend to End Breast Cancer. This is a 60-kilometre walk through Toronto on a Saturday and Sunday to raise money for Princess Margaret Hospital's research, diagnostic, treatment, and support programs for breast-cancer patients. Kathy was tireless in her efforts to raise money for this event. She was successful in achieving her goal of $5000 in donations! She walked the 30K on Saturday, camped overnight in a little blue tent, then got up and walked another 30K on Sunday. A fantastic accomplishment, considering Kathy's feet had been affected by her chemo, but she was a trooper. At one point, I looked at her and saw the strength that she was drawing from the thousands who were out that weekend to support the cause. I know it gave her great hope that new treatments were just around the corner.

Kathy was such an advocate for the cause of breast cancer research, prevention, and, ultimately, a cure! She was the team leader for the Warriors of Hope Breast Cancer Survivor Dragon Boat Team in The Run for The Cure. Top fundraiser for the city, she helped our team be the top fundraising team in North Bay. Kathy would impress upon us how important it was for us to do our part in the community and, by her efforts, she inspired us to do better! No doubt about it.

In the dragon boat, she knew what it was like to paddle from all corners. She paddled in the front, in the middle, in the back. She paddled on the right, she paddled on the left; wherever she was needed, that is where she would paddle! And when she was unable to paddle, she would be our drummer. Wasn't that a magnificent photo of Kathy, 'Triumphant Drummer,' that was on display at her visitation?

After my very first out-of-town race in 2000, I was so euphoric and felt so empowered by the whole experience that I could not sleep that night. I got up and put pen to paper and wrote a short poem. The last few lines read:

We slip into the lake in our dragon boat Jane
Our bodies bursting with the joy of life, forgetting all past pain
For this hour we exchange the battle for the paddle
Fierce hope in our every stroke
I am strong. I am proud. I am a Warrior of Hope.

In the last few years, Kathy did indeed exchange her battle for the paddle each time she got into that boat. And she did it with great enthusiasm. Within the next few weeks, we will once again slip into the lake in our dragon boat, Jane. When our coach says, "Paddles up. Take it away", I just know that Kathy's presence will be felt by us all and we will all have a much fiercer hope in our every stroke! Kathy, simply put, was one awesome Warrior of Hope! Bye for now Kathy, we will miss you terribly.

Shelley Loponen, on behalf of the Warriors of Hope

Joe Hargrave

First, I would like to start by telling you that I met my hero a long time ago and he knew, from the start, that we were going to play important roles in each other's lives. I will begin at the end when I found myself standing in front of a packed funeral home, speaking of this man, the extremely tough job he chose to do, and the impact he had on me.

One line from my prepared and rehearsed speech was, "anyone who had ever met him, liked him, even with his daily grind filled with stress and challenges." To me, life is about situations and how you choose to deal with them, and this man instilled in me the confidence to deal with anything. Thankfully, this individual stayed in my life and helped me enjoy a successful life of my own. This man happened to be my father and had one of the most difficult and demanding jobs in the world, that of being a dad for the rest of his life.

I believe times were different 40 or so years ago, when there was not as much focus placed on material items or trophies - like the new car to show your neighbours. There were, however, the constant demands, challenges and rewards of being a parent. My hero never dropped me off at the arena or ball field. He took me, watched me and rarely instructed but rather encouraged me to do the best I could. I realize I came along a little later than my brother and sisters, so he had prior training and I feel blessed for that.

Without his guidance, I would not be the person I am today and I find myself trying extremely hard to be half the man he was, so my son, daughter and wife can have the best life they can. It is the circle of life. I am the father trying very hard to be Dad.

It is now years since my dad passed on and now I realize how much of a hero he was to me. A father does not have to buy his children's love for the time he is not able to spend with them; rather, a dad will gladly spend the time to enjoy his family. We sometimes get caught up in a race to have it all when, most of the time, we already have 'it'; we just can't take the time to see it. A child needs the love of parents. Thankfully, I had two loving parents. Now that I am a dad, I realize I have a job for the rest of my life; one my hero did and did better than anyone I know.

Terry *Hargrave*

Milton Wallace Smith

His name was Milton Wallace Smith and he was my father. He was born into a family with an alcoholic father who was incapable of keeping a job. There were five brothers and two sisters who shared a similar fate. The one bright spot in their lives was their mother, Laura, who kept the family together, despite her little means. In 1933, what little world they had came crashing down as their mother lost her life. A large goitre had grown from her neck, due to a lack of salt, and it took her life.

Their father, in true fashion, left the children and they had to fend for themselves. In those days, money was tight as they were in the midst of the Great Depression. Dad told me that it was in those years that he learned the value of family. He had to take his younger brother, Ross, by the hand and give him away to Aunt Hattie and Uncle George to raise, separate from the rest of the siblings. They, too, had very little. Ross was just six years old. My father had to labour on a farm for no more than room and board, and Dad said the farmer was a very hard man to work for. He toiled away until he was nothing more than skin and bones.

With nowhere to turn, he continued on with his plight. My dad always knew the value of education and continued to read anything that would help him. Dad eventually had to go to work for another farmer, but things did not improve. His appendix ruptured and he laid all night in the pouring rain and nearly lost his life, but was taken to the hospital and survived. The nurses felt sorry for him and kept him in the hospital for as long as they could. No one paid the bill, nor did papa visit.

After that, he went to a family member and lived in a heated shed in the back of the house. There was food so, for a time, he could attend school. He took full advantage of this opportunity. He became an entrepreneur and he owned a gas station in Cameron, Ontario, with his brother. He had an ambition of relocating his family out of the village to the small town of Lindsay. When I was six years old, we made the big move and he became the first person in Lindsay to have his own business and to own a digger, which he worked at for a few years. Eventually, he studied to become a fourth class stationary engineer and landed a job at Ross Memorial Hospital, where he worked until his retirement at the age of 62.

My father taught me some very important lessons and these lessons I truly cherish. He always knew the importance of money and managed it very well. Dad said it was nice to be important, but more important to be nice. He was never vain and never tried to impress anyone. If someone got a new car, he would say, "That's alright. Be happy for them." He loved and raised three children with what he had and was fiercely independent. These singular qualities made him a special father, an amazing grandfather, a favourite uncle, and a true friend.

Gail Samuel

William 'Bill' Oliver

I could write about so many things that William 'Bill' Oliver had done, but what got me more was what he would say. Some things, I'm certain, I cannot write. He would use little sayings or phrases he picked up. To my grandmother, they were rude, somewhat vulgar, disgusting expressions. To me, though, they were a driving force.

I am not a religious person but I believe there is something higher up than we are. My 'gramps' was the same. He had a saying which he meant no harm by, which went, "Jim, you gotta win. Why? The Lord hates a loser!" Vulgar? Maybe to some. Not to me. He knew what it would take to get me to follow my dreams.

Sadly, a few years back, my grandpa got sick and passed away. At his funeral, all of his family was there. It was amazing. My cousin gave the eulogy and, not that it wasn't good, but I felt I needed to say something, so I did. I told everyone what a great man he was and that he had done so much for me and many of the people out there. There was something I wish I could have done and regret not doing and, up until a year ago, I didn't know why. Before my grandpa passed, he talked to me and asked me what I wanted to be. I thought and thought and I came up with 'actor'. I honestly had no idea. He smiled at me and said, "Actor, huh, well." Then under his breath, with his eyes looking up, he said, "Lord, he is not a loser.' Then he smiled at me.

Until a while ago, I really thought the idea of my being an actor was a joke, but then I finished my first play and it went well. The second-term play was coming up and I was hesitant. I don't know why; I just was. I auditioned, got a lead, and then about two weeks in, I quit. In my head, I was done with acting, but I don't know why. I quit and I was done. Grandpa would have been disappointed. Two days before the opening night of the play, a girl from the cast ran into my class and said, "Jim! James (my understudy) got hit by a car!" I know, insane. So, with two days and the phrase, "The Lord hates a loser" burning in my head, I took the part and had an amazing show. Since then, I've been acting . . . good acting! So, what I wanted to say that I couldn't in my eulogy is just, 'Thank you!'

Jim Watson

Shirley Duschesne
(Before She Left)

The deadliest disease took her away from us. We found out about this tragedy around the beginning of December, 2004. It was the most horrifying day of my life. My Aunt Shirley was the world to me. I must have spent half of my life with her.

About every other weekend when I was young, she would pick me up for a sleepover. Before we went to her house, she would take me to the mall. She would always buy me something new. It would be either a toy or clothes. While we were out, she would usually take me to McDonalds for dinner, but we would go through the drive-thru. We did this so we could go home and eat our dinner while watching a movie. We never had anything planned. We would just go with the flow and have a great time.

My aunt's cottage was my favourite place in the world. I felt like I was free out there. I remember the time when my whole family was there. My brother had gotten a leech stuck to his foot while he was swimming. Ever since that incident, I was afraid to go in that water. I also had a pet squirrel out there and his name was Chippy. He would always be on the patio in the morning, waiting for his peanuts. I loved being at the cottage. It was like my second home.

My aunt was a nurse. I remember the one time she took me to work with her, before she had to drop me off at home. She told me that I could join her only if I was on my best behaviour, so I promised and I had so much fun watching my aunt work. One of my aunt's patients made dolls for a profession. She made me a doll and named it Alice-May, which was my great-grandmother's name. My aunt told me that I couldn't have the doll until she was not with us anymore. I still have the doll and I will cherish it forever.

I guess you could say that my aunt and I were as close as two peas in a pod. When my little cousin was born, we turned into three peas in a pod. We were all so close and did so much together. I helped my aunt take care of my cousin. I didn't spend as much time then with my aunt as I did before my cousin was born. This was only because my cousin was my aunt's only granddaughter and I wanted to give my cousin a chance to get what I had, when I was her age.

When my aunt was put into the hospital for the first time, I couldn't stop crying. I was always worried about her and always afraid of losing her when I was not there. I realized that we might not have as much time together as I thought we would. I was soon informed that she would be alright. She got to go home and spend as much time as she could with my cousin and me.

After my aunt's first trip to the hospital, she started to slow down. This was because she was on chemotherapy. She was tired and wasn't herself anymore. Even my little cousin had noticed. She tried her hardest to keep up with us and do everything she used to, but she just couldn't do it. Whenever she was having a good day, my cousin and I would be there.

Soon, she had to go back to the hospital. This time, I didn't think she would be going home. She just didn't look good. She had her surgery, but it didn't work. She was getting sicker every day. The doctors knew it was almost the end and they couldn't do anything more for her, so they moved her to a room at the opposite end of the hallway from the Critical Care Unit. I knew exactly what it meant. After the long battle, she was tired and finally went to heaven, peacefully.

Aunt Shirley had more courage than anybody I know. She was a fighter and never gave up on anything. She taught me so much that I needed to know about life. If she had not been there for me, I would not be the person I am today. She showed me how to be a wonderful and charming person, just like her. She did so much for me and taught me to always think before I act. When I am in a bad situation, I will always say, "What would Aunty Shirley do?" Many people think she is just gone, but to me she will always be here.

Allie Spilchuk, 14

George Tougas
(Gone but Not Forgotten - My Father)

Today is Tuesday, April 3, 2007, and it would have been my father's 87th birthday, but three years ago, he lost his courageous battle with cancer. After visiting his remains at St. Mary's Cemetery, I felt compelled to acknowledge my father as the biggest role model in my life.

My father wasn't famous or well-educated. Growing up during the Great Depression, my father was forced to work at an early age and his education was limited to grade eight. Working for most of his life, his world was committed to his five children and to my mother, to whom he was married for close to 60 years. Now that I have lived and worked for over 25 years, I feel extremely fortunate to have been raised by strong parents. My father wasn't well-educated, but was extremely wise. I still catch myself paraphrasing him to my family and students/athletes. Comments like, "I'm not smarter than you, but just more experienced", is one of my favourites.

One time, as a youth, I questioned his parenting skills and he quickly fired back, "Well, son, I guess we will have to see how well you will do as a parent". Once again, he was right. Parenting is the most difficult thing you can do in life. Probably one of the greatest gifts he gave me was the opportunity to enjoy my youth. Even though we were not affluent, we never went without in our lives. My passion was sports and, in his wisdom, he told me, "You are going to work for the rest of your life so we will find a way for you to play."

Many kids miss out on education and extra-curricular activities because they have to work. I think my involvement in activities created the framework of my character and established me for my future endeavours. Many people who knew my father come to me and are quick to comment how much they miss him and how it is not the same because he is no longer alive. In our society, we sometimes tend to worship movie stars, politicians, and athletes but the real heroes are the people that touch our lives every day that they are, or were, on earth. When my father died on June 24th, 2004, he had dwindled down to 100 pounds. Cancer may have taken his body away from us, but it didn't affect his soul and didn't affect his teachings that will remain with me for the rest of my life. Thanks, Dad!

Larry Tougas

CHAPTER SIX

OUR GRADE ONES

Once I'm done kindergarten, I'm going to find me a wife.

Tommy - Age 5

Mrs. Attema

My hero is Mrs. Attema. She is my hero because she taught me how to write and draw. Now, I love to write and draw. I have my own writing desk at my house. I have a printer, too. She is my teacher. She is one of my favourite teachers because she is nice to me and she knows my brother too. Mrs. Attema is a teacher at Vincent Massey. She teaches grade one and that is my grade. She lives in a straw house and she saves power and that is good for the environment. She drives a small car so she doesn't pollute the air. I am nice to her. She is my hero because she is helping to make the world a better place to live.

Emily Drenth

Rosey and Orville Feltz
(Huggable Heroes)

When I first thought of heroes, I thought of superheroes with superpowers. In this case, they are really nice people who never forget their family. My heroes are my grandma and grandpa. They are great because they never fight when I am there. They brought money into the community.

Travis Feltz

Bubby Rose Goldfarb

I never met my Bubby Rose but I'm named after her. She was my dad's mom and she is my hero. When the Second World War started she was ten years old. All the Jewish people were forced to live together in a small part of town called a ghetto. Rose lived in the ghetto with her mom and dad and eight brothers and sisters. There wasn't much food and life was hard, and it was going to get harder.

The Nazis sent the people in the ghetto away. First they sent away the little children and the old people. They put them on cattle cars on the trains and no one ever saw them again. Next they came and took everyone else.

My Bubby Rose was sent to a concentration camp. At the death camp my Bubby Rose and two of her sisters were picked to go in one line. The rest of her family was sent to a different line and they were never seen again.

Next Bubby Rose and her sisters were sent to a slave labour camp. They worked on building a runway. My Bubby Rose got very sick with typhoid fever. Luckily, just when things were at their worst, the American soldiers liberated my Bubby Rose and her sisters.

She traveled to Canada with her sisters. She lived in Montreal. She met my Zayda who lived in Toronto. They got married and she moved away from her sisters to live in

Toronto. She had two sons; my daddy and my uncle David. They had a very happy life together.

My Bubby Rose died of cancer in 1991. My mommy and daddy say that she would have been the best bubby ever. I think she is the best hero.

Rose Goldfarb

Dr. Karen Morris

Hi! My name is Hannah. My hero is my dentist because she pulls my teeth out when they are loose and when she pulls them out, it does not hurt. She takes x-rays of my teeth and gums. My dentist also cleans my teeth and makes them shiny. My dentist is also my aunt and she checks my teeth for cavities and, so far, I have no cavities yet. She tells my mom when to come back to her office. When I leave, she gives me a toy.

Hannah Irwin

Jody Stockfish

Hi, my name is Sarah. My hero is my Aunt Jody. My Aunt Jody helps lots of animals. She writes lots of stories for her magazines. She loves to help animals. She rescued dogs that people had been mean to. She really looked after them well and they were happy. They lived a long life. One of her dogs is still here, but the other one has died. She volunteers her time to help at lots of animal shelters. She is a hero for lots of animals.

Sarah Irwin

Jim Jordan

My dad is my hero because he saved my day. I'll tell you how he saved my day. There was a frozen lake. I fell into it. I was lucky that my dad pulled me out and saved my day.

Brent Jordan

Karen Manning

My mom is my hero because she feeds me dinner and takes me to my friend's house. She takes me to school and she is nice to me. She takes me to bed and she helps me do my homework. She is nice to my friends and she lets me invite friends over to my house. She is nice to her kids and her pets and she takes care of me.

Sara Manning

My Four Heroes

Hi. I have four heroes. They are my aunt, my brother, my mom, and my teacher. My teacher's name is Mrs. Attema. All my heroes are nice. My aunt helps when she takes Jacob off of me when he is hitting me. My brother helps me when I'm scared at plays. My mom helps me when I am sick and my teacher is my hero because she makes me write and now I love writing. I love it and that's why they are my heroes.

Maiya Nevrencan

God

God is my hero because he gave me a healthy body and he loves me and he protects me. He makes me be good at school.

Marshall Point

Syeda Gilani

My hero is my mommy because she takes care of me and she does everything for me. She cooks dinner, lunch, and breakfast for me. She changes my clothes for me. She is nice to me. She is really good to me. She tells me what to do. What makes her a hero is that she loves me. And I love her.

Zainab Razaly

Cameron Buckle

My hero is my Uncle Cam because he was a firefighter. How many people do you think he saved? As a fireman in San Francisco, California, he has saved many lives and has put out lots of big fires. Uncle Cam also worked on a fireboat so he rescued people from San Francisco Bay. He is really helpful because he fixes things for my granny and he is a very good cook. When he visits, he has lots of fun playing sports and watching TV with me.

Brennan Richardson

Hannah Irwin
(A Good Friend)

My hero is Hannah Irwin because she saved a caterpillar from the lake and it was drowning. Hannah is also my hero because she helps me when I am hurt and she is my hero because she is a very good friend.

Hana Ryan

Dr. Steven Steinberg

My hero is my doctor because when I am sick, he will help me. My doctor is very nice. His name is Doctor Steinberg.

Shaye Stephenson

Sandra Stewart

My hero is my mom because she inspired me to like planting and that takes a long time. That taught me to take my time and I always do. I'm glad that, in different ways, my mom taught me that I should take my time. I really am glad my mom did that for me. That's why my mom is my hero.

Jennifer Stewart

Trevor Thomas

My favourite hero is my dad because my uncle was drowning and he saved him.

Sydney Thomas

Mrs. Attema

My hero is Mrs. Attema because she teaches us how to read, she saves the environment and, also, because she writes amazing books. Instead of spraying the flowers, she puts them in her salad. Mrs. Attema is a great book writer and a great teacher. Mrs. Attema wrote many books.

Giulia Valenti

CHAPTER SEVEN

OUR MILITARY

When a soldier steps on foreign soil in a high-risk environment, every single Canadian should be walking with him or her.

Rick Hillier

Walter Marshall

Poppy, as my sister and I called him, was born in the province of Newfoundland; however, it was not a province of
Canada back then. He grew up not having much and that is
how he lived most of his life. He always made the best of
what he had, no matter how little there was. When war broke
out in 1939, Poppy signed up with the Newfoundland Navy,
a branch of Great Britain's Royal Navy. He was discharged
from the Navy in 1945 and returned home to Dunnville,
Newfoundland. Soon after his long voyages at sea ended, he
had his first child, his only daughter and my aunt, Ruth
Marshall. Shortly after that, he had four sons: Paul, Don (my
dad), John, and Frank. After the last child was born, con-
frontation arose between my grandfather and grandmother.
My grandma left my grandpa, alone with five children in the
poor province of Newfoundland.

Walter worked jobs with minimal income just to pay the
bills and make ends meet. For years and years, he worked
long hours, then came home from work and cooked and
cleaned. Even up until shortly before he died, Walter went
out into the forest and chopped wood each day for the
wood stove. My uncle Paul was mentally handicapped so
taking care of him was a full time job as well. My uncle died
at the age of 21, after his brain ruptured. The family was
devastated but, in some ways, relieved. He had gone to a
better place and no one had to worry about his future when
everyone would move on. My grandpa was there every single day for Paul and every other member of the family. He

was also a very wise man. He said such things as, "Do not mourn for people when they die; you should celebrate their life. If you mourn, it means that they did not lead a good life, but if you celebrate, they know that they left behind the happiness that their life was filled with."

I never grew tired of talking to my grandpa on the phone. I did it at least once a week. He always had interesting stories to tell me and I felt honoured to talk to such a great man. Every Christmas, he would send my sister and me a present. It was never anything big, but it meant so much. This man had barely enough money to feed himself and he was still looking after my uncles, John and Frank, who were still living at home; yet he still sent us a present for Christmas and our birthdays, every year.

The Christmas of 2000 was one that changed my life forever. A few months before, Poppy was diagnosed with cancer. At 9 a.m. on Christmas morning of 2000, my family received a call from my Aunt Ruth saying that he had just passed at the age of 83. I was completely devastated. Although I had never met him, he meant the world to me. He would have done anything for my family or anyone else close to him, because he was just that kind of person. No matter how little Poppy had, it would go to others, before him. The funeral was held in Newfoundland and there wasn't enough money for all of us to go, considering it was Christmas, so my sister and I stayed at my grandparents' house in Brantford, Ontario. Poppy served his country and family with the utmost distinction and passion. I just wish I could have said goodbye in person.

Steve Marshall, 15

Moofa

Dear Moofa,

This is a picture of you sailing. I hope you are having fun. See you soon. Lots of love,

Jesse

I wrote this letter to my grandfather, whom my younger sister and I call Moofa. I wrote it at the same time he taught me how to tie my shoes using 'the Moofa knot'. When I tied my shoes using the Moofa knot, they never, ever came undone.

Moofa was born in Buenos Aires in 1912 and lived there until he was seven. He then moved with his family to Norway, just before World War I ended. When he was only 16, Moofa worked on a ship and traveled all around the world. After World War II, Moofa left everything behind in Norway and moved to Canada.

Moofa has always had a love for sailing. He sailed in the 1932 Summer Olympics, winning a silver medal for Norway. He also qualified for the 1936 Winter Olympics in downhill racing. The Olympics were cancelled due to some problems before World War II. He told me a story about when he was introduced to someone as "Norway's best skier". Moofa was also passionate about cross-country skiing. He would go into the woods and make his own paths. My love for sailing, downhill skiing and cross-country has definitely come from Moofa.

In World War II, Moofa was a spitfire pilot in the Royal Air Force. He came to Canada to train with the Royal Norwegian Air Force and then went overseas to fight with the Royal Air Force. During the war, Moofa got a bullet through one of his knees and also had a bomb go off right by his ear, leaving him deaf. Moofa was so brave to give up everything, even knowing the risks he was going to take, just to fight for his country. He would always tell me stories about when he was in the war. He would show me pictures and just talk about different things he experienced.

Moofa accomplished many things throughout his life. He won a medal in the Olympics, he fought for his country and was brave during everything. When he moved to Canada, he left everything behind and was ready to start a new life in yet another country.

Moofa is now 94 years old and he lives in a retirement home. Only the little things in life are what matter to Moofa now, like the Tim Horton's coffee and pecan danish we bring when we go to visit. Huge things like getting a medal in the Olympics and risking his life to fight in a war don't matter to Moofa at all anymore. He has done more in his life than I could ever do in two lives. I know Moofa won't be alive forever, but I will always love him.

Jesse Cameron, 16

Jess Larochelle

Jess Larochelle, my friend's son, joined the Canadian Forces and trained as a soldier. He became a sharp-shooter and was stationed in Afghanistan in August, 2006.

In October, he was on duty at an outpost while his company guarded other troops who were building roads. They came under fire and Jess' outpost was hit by a rocket-propelled grenade. He was blown out of the post and knocked unconscious. He came to, only to hear his commander yelling, "Larochelle's dead." He wondered to himself, "Am I really dead?"

He picked himself up and got back in the damaged post. He went from one gun to another, providing covering fire on either side of the post. He held off 20 Taliban attackers and saved their position from being overrun. His commander later stated that had he not been able to hold the post, they would have been overrun and would have suffered many more casualties. Two men lost their lives in that attack, but Jess saved many from the same fate.

He returned to camp and helped carry his buddy's casket to the plane the next day. Only after that did he admit he was hurt and allow the doctors to have a look. He had damage to two vertebrae in his neck and was sent home for treatment, trying to avoid spinal surgery. He is now on light duty, hoping to return to active duty in Afghanistan.

He has been awarded the Star of Valour, Canada's highest military honour next to the Victoria Cross.

Cheryl Hughes

Doug Hermeston

I learned the news over the phone - not the greatest way to be told of a death in the family almost a week after Christmas. It was expected, of course. My grandfather had been battling cancer for over three years; yet, it was still sudden. It's always sudden.

The year was 2001, a day before 2002. My New Year's Eve party was spent on a Greyhound bus returning home, the countdown taking place somewhere about 200 kilometres from North Bay. I didn't count down. I didn't feel like it. My grandfather was dead and I wasn't there.

He always made me laugh. He would go across to Pine Hill Coffee Shop and hit on the younger women, sometimes just to get a rise out of grandmother. His last birthday, the women at Buns Master Bakery had set up a sign in their window, wishing him a good one; their window was directly across the road and it made the whole family smile. He even gave me a speech on the difference between our version of space and time. That's from my memory as a 15-year-old boy. That's what made him my hero; he barely had to try.

Then I grew a bit older and, after his death, I learned the true version of war. I study about World War II and realize the horrors inflicted on the brave soldiers of the past. I see now that when they came home, they lived harder lives because of their experiences, never fully overcoming them. The pride I had for my grandfather grew. He fought in Word War II. He defended his country and others, always with his life on the line, to give the world the freedom it enjoys today.

After the war, he came home, being lucky enough to be one who survived. He married my grandmother and helped the baby boom out a bit by giving the world nine children, the youngest being my mother. He made sure there was always food on the table and found a job, which I learned wasn't the easiest task for soldiers returning. He was haunted by many ghosts that weren't there, the price he had to pay for his noble deeds. Victory is always bitter-sweet, though in war, there never really is a thing such as victory.

We always see others in a new light after they die. We go through grieving and sometimes the images of those we see are not those we like to admit to, but as a boy, all I knew was that I was going to miss him and that I loved him.

In memory of Doug Hermeston
1921 to 2001

Matt St.Onge

Doug McDonald

My name is Vern Mortson and I am a transplant from Kirkland Lake. My hero is the late Doug McDonald. He was a friend to everyone and everyone's friend. In his earlier days, Doug coached, played and refereed hockey and was respected in all aspects of the game.

He served his country in the Second World War and retired as a colonel. He was a member of the Canadian Legion, Branch 23, and a distinguished member of the Rotary Club. He taught many people in North Bay how to drive. In everything he did, Doug was liked and respected. He sponsored many sports activities in North Bay. In 1995, I started skating with the 'Seniors and Tots' and got to know Doug as a man who went out of his way to help people. It was amazing to me that Doug still skated with us, into his 92nd year. He was an inspiration to all who skated with him. Doug is no longer with us. He was a man who gave freely of his time and talents for his city and country, without seeking any reward. May God bless you, Doug.

Vern Mortson

Ian Cowan

Ian Cowan has inspired me throughout my life and continues to do so today. He has led an incredible and interesting life and yet, he still wants more. He has seen many things, been many places, and is now making a difference in a small city in Northern Ontario.

Ian was born in Toronto, Ontario, but lived there only a short time. He was the first child of Jim, a Korean war veteran, and Betty Cowan. Jim was a general in the Canadian Armed Forces, so they moved a lot: Germany, England, India (where Ian's little brother and my uncle, Scott, was born), and Kansas. You name the place and they've visited it at least once. When Ian turned 18, he followed in his father's footsteps and joined the military. He went to flight school and learned how to fly jets. He jumped out of airplanes, went on peacekeeping missions and built schools in Honduras and Nicaragua. He experienced army life to the fullest and he decided to go to medical school to become a doctor for the military. He met his future wife and my mom, Judy, and got married a few years later. They had me a few years after that and we were posted to the city of North Bay after living in Calgary, Ottawa, and Barrie.

He worked at CFB North Bay as a doctor for four years before my sister was born. He had worked enough years in the military for a full pension and he decided it was time to get out. He retired a major and decided to work as a civilian doctor. Ian, Dr. Rick Senior (my uncle), Dr. Mike Leckie, and Dr. Joel Carter decided to form the Northgate Medical Clinic. The clinic has added three new doctors and given many medical students the experience to go and get a job elsewhere. He also works at the hospital and he knows so many people, it's scary. Wherever he walks, someone says, "Hello, Dr. Cowan." It's one of those things that is really cool but really weird, since I don't know most of them.

Before we had career day at Chippewa, I never really appreciated how hard my dad works. He works 80 hours every week for 48 weeks of the year. Most people don't realize how hard, and how much, he works. He also constantly thinks of others. I went on a fishing trip with him and we were the only boat that hadn't caught a fish. After three hours of fishing, his rod got a bite and instead of him reeling it in, he let me catch it. The fish turned out to be the biggest fish caught by anyone that day. For that and countless other reasons, my dad is my hero.

Chris Cowan, 15

Albert Starka

My grandpa survived some pretty dangerous stuff. He fought in World War II, badly hurt his ears in a gold mine, survived a mini heart attack, and died of one.

He fought in World War II to help his country. He was only 17 years old. The country he fought in was Austria. After the war, he came to Canada by ship and then he worked in a gold mine. While he was working at the mine, his ears got really badly hurt by all the noises. After he hurt his ears, he couldn't hear very well so when I talked to him on the phone, I had to speak loudly and clearly so that he could hear most of it.

Grandpa had some pretty painful heart attacks that he didn't know about. On Friday, March 2, 2007, my dad told my mom that my grandpa had died. When me and my mom heard, we cried and cried but Kole, my 4-year old brother, didn't have any idea what was going on, so he wasn't crying. After my hero died, everything changed, like Grandma lives alone and my mom can no longer talk to or see her dad, and I no longer have a grandpa to see or talk to.

My hero is the best hero in the world. He will always remain in my heart and he was 82 when he died.

Kasey Mishquart, 9

Abe and Olive Joseph

There were five girls, our mom, and our dad. The first miracle was when my dad's parents fled Poland and went to Glasgow, Scotland, where my dad was born. They booked a passage on a ship but, because my grandmother was ill, they waited for another time - and missed taking the Titanic. They immigrated to Canada the following year, lived in Toronto for a couple of years, and then headed to North Bay. My grandparents' last name was difficult to pronounce and when they came to Canada, it was changed. My father is now Joseph Abraham Joseph.

He was a nice looking young man with black, curly hair. He was very quiet, shy, and blushed easily, I am told. He didn't mention having many girlfriends, but that was to change when his brother's girlfriend, Daisy, asked him to call her friend, Olive Franklin. He did decide to call but when he went to pick her up, he almost changed his mind and left. He gathered his courage, went to the door, and it was love at first sight. This is when my family started.

Dad enlisted in the air force in 1940. Even though he had never flown, he wanted to be a pilot. He was sent to Brandon, Manitoba, to train, graduated as a sergeant pilot, and was sent to Pat Bay where he began a career as a flying-boat pilot. My mom and my sister, Judith, traveled by train to be with him. My mom had great memories of friends she met out there. Dad was then posted to Bella Bella, where he was considered to be the best pilot in the squadron, flying PBYs,

Cats, and Cansos. He was promoted to the rank of flight officer and was awarded the Operational Wings and the Pacific Star. They patrolled day in and day out, up to 16 hours a day, as Japanese subs were shelling their radar installations.

Miracle number two happened in August, 1943, when their Canso left on an extra long patrol, but ran into fog and lost contact with the surface. The aircraft, weighted down with a heavy load of fuel, was unable to climb above the fog. It lost altitude and was about to crash into the side of a mountain. Dad knew they were going to hit and at that moment he acted instinctively and cut the throttle and pulled the control column to his stomach. He remembers the terrific force, the heat, and the moans of his crew. The impact killed his flight engineer and he ordered the remaining eight to escape through the front windshield. He can still visualize the sights, smells, and sounds today. Years later, he realized he had cracked the base of his spine.

In 1945, he took his discharge and because of a promise he had made at home, he returned. By this time there were two daughters and I believe my mom was expecting me. It was a hard decision for them to return home as they really loved the west coast and the people they had met.

We had a wonderful family life. As far back as I can remember, we were so lucky to have these special parents. My mom and dad enjoyed traveling with us, fishing and boating, camping, and square dancing. Both became master bowlers. We all took dance lessons and mom made us the most beautiful costumes. There were so many wonderful times and fond memories, too many to mention.

They both worked until 1980 when the family retired. They were married for just over 65 years. My mom passed away in December 2004, leaving my dad devastated. She was always very protective of him and I think he always thought that, because of their age difference, he would be the first to go.

In February 2007, my dad turned 96. He still goes to his Hall of Famers luncheons at the 406 Wing. He is a member of the Legion. In 2005, he was one of the veterans of the year. He was very honoured but wished mom was still here to see the veterans praised. He has so many friends and acquaintances that speak so highly of him.

Dad is a quiet, gentle soul who recalls his years in the Royal Canadian Air Force with fondness. He treasures the memory of many lost friends and comrades. When he talks of our mom, he brings tears to my eyes. They have 14 grandchildren, 17 great-grandchildren and one great-great-grandchild. We love you mom and dad. You're our miracles.

Sherry Sullivan

Kristian Youmans

Ever since he was little, Kristian has been dyslexic and had the hardest time in school. He struggled in all grades until he arrived at W.J. Fricker. There, a special teacher realized that Kristian needed help before he entered high school and decided to tutor him. My mom also worked with him each day.

Kristian learned a lot by the time he reached Grade 12. He was a very talented young man who loved repairing broken objects, just to see if he could make them work again. The best part of it was that he was great at it! After Kristian graduated, he decided to pursue a career in the navy. Kristian told us that he wanted to join the military, but was nervous because of an entrance exam he needed to pass in order to be accepted. Kristian studied his heart out and took his exam. My mom and I were probably just as nervous as he was. When Kristian called to tell us his results, we were on edge. It turned out that, out of 63 people writing the exam, he had gotten the second highest score!

He proved to me then that all of the tutoring and hard work to achieve his goals really did pay off. My brother has now been in the navy for six years and is working his way up the ladder. He is a Marine Engineer Technician and he loves it. Kristian is also a Gulf War veteran (the current one) as he spent nine months overseas, and all by the age of 25. I am so proud of my brother and I love him very much.

Sarah Youmans, 14

Colby Ricker
(My WWII Survivor)

During World War II, Colby Ricker's task was to operate the tanks. Then one day, during an explosion, he was shot in the leg and wounded. Though he is a very strong man, it took him a while to recuperate from his wounds. Nevertheless, he is up and walking today. He is 90 years old and still living in the same house for the last 50 years, with some help from his three daughters.

After he got married to Natalie Ricker, they had three children together. They raised them to the best of their abilities and they each turned out to be amazing people. They are all at his house right now and they are all helping him out with anything he needs. They pretty much live with him now. About five years ago, his wife passed away and he was devastated. No one thought he would be able to survive without the companionship of his wife but, wouldn't you know it, he is still alive today and fighting strong.

About one year after finishing his duties in the war, he was awarded the Purple Heart Medal and everyone was so proud of him because he served his country well. I remember the last time I was at his house, he hung it up on the wall in the living room so he could show everyone what he had done to serve and protect his country.

This summer, my family and I will be going on our annual vacation to Wells, Maine, to visit him. I expect to see him fighting as strong as usual. Though he is sick, he manages to spend some quality time with us, even though it might not be a lot. So when I am down in Maine this year for my vacation, I will not be looking forward to swimming in the ocean, going to the arcades, or playing on the beach. I will be looking forward to spending my time with my Grampy Ricker.

Brandon Baril, 15

David Byers

My Hero is David Byers because he went to the war and saved most people's lives. He didn't get to say goodbye to his mom and dad because he died.

Cora Patterson, 6

CHAPTER EIGHT

OUR GRANDMOTHERS

Grandma always made you feel she had been waiting to see - just you - all day and now the day was complete.

Marcy DeMaree

Peggy Clarke

Hello, my name is Dakota Jodouin. My grandma, Peggy Clarke, was present when I was born. As I grew and grew, Grandma was there. She would pick me up every Friday and I would stay the weekends with her. She took me to lots of places. My favorite place was British Columbia, to visit my cousins.

The thing that makes her my hero is that she has never made a promise to me that she hasn't kept, no matter how big or how small. Grandma has been to all of my soccer and hockey games. She even came to Vincent Massey to have lunch with me when my mother couldn't. She sleeps over when my mom is on early shift and makes my lunch and puts special things in it. She gets me and my sister off to daycare before she goes to work. Sometimes, she is late for work because I have a hard time getting up in the morning. She makes up silly songs and games to wake us up. We like the sillier, the better.

Grandma reads me bedtime stories and never forgets to make my bed in the morning. Grandma has the best sleepovers with pop, chips and dip, movies, and staying up late. My grandpa is away a lot, so I like to protect grandma by being the man that keeps her safe.

My grandmother always lets me use her computer and she always takes my side when things go wrong. She listens and helps me problem-solve to figure out the best answers. She enjoys helping me with my homework. She never gets tired of giving hugs and kisses. She loves to give bear-hugs and cuddles on the couch.

Grandma is my best friend. Thank you for being my grandma. I love you to the moon and back, and as far as a motorcycle can travel.

Love, your beaner,
Dakota Jodouin, 7

Dr. Renée Porter

What would you expect to be doing at the age of 66? You would probably think that you would be well into living out your retirement plans. I'm sure you would never picture yourself walking across a stage at Convocation Hall at the University of Toronto, receiving your doctorate degree, but that is exactly what Renée Porter did.

Renée was born in a small outport in Newfoundland called Kings Point. She was the second child of Salvation Army minister parents. She spent her childhood, during the Depression, moving with her family from small town to small town, helping the community through their church work.

In Newfoundland in the 1930's, life was very simple and she was educated in a one-room schoolhouse. She didn't have the luxury of having indoor plumbing or electricity and, because she was a woman, any dreams that required an education weren't much of a possibility.

Desiring a career, Renée decided to go to school to become a registered nurse. She married and moved to Toronto in order to further her husband's education. After having two girls, she decided to be a stay-at-home mother. While raising her children and working as a part-time nurse, her hidden dream of pursuing her education returned and she enrolled at the University of Toronto and obtained her Bachelor of Arts degree. Fifteen courses and 10 years later, at the age of 47, she graduated with her B.A.

The stimulation and thrill of accomplishing her goal spurred her on and she began to work on her Bachelor of Science in nursing. After three more years, she completed that degree, even having to go back one of those years full-time. This gave her an opportunity to get a teaching job at Seneca College Nursing School. Renée didn't stop there. She decided to work on a Masters of Education. She actually graduated with the same degree in the same year as her older daughter.

After all that schooling, you would think that Renée would have been happy to sit back and relax, but she started to work on her doctorate on a part-time basis. She completed her doctorate in 1992, at the age of 66, debt free.

Renée Porter, or Nana as I call her, is my hero because she had a dream and she fulfilled it. She is an amazing example of someone who doesn't let obstacles, gender, or age limit her dreams.

Kara Beadle, 14

Joan Fraser
(a.k.a. Grandma Hugs)

Some people think that you have to have muscles like musclemen or spin webs like Spiderman to be a hero, but you don't. My grandma is my hero and she doesn't have any powers. She is my hero because she fought cancer, she was loyal to me and my family and she raised a child with brain problems.

To begin with, my grandma got cancer when she was in her 70's. She was in the hospital for over a year and fought cancer for a long time. Cancer made my grandma so weak that she couldn't open her eyes. At Christmas, we went to sing Christmas carols. My grandma tried to clap but she couldn't. She died on Boxing Day, 2005.

Every year my grandma would come to our house from Kingston (that is six hours away) for our birthdays and special occasions. That means that she would come to our house about 10 times a year. My grandma would always read us stories from the Bible and come with us to church.

The last way my grandma is my hero is because she raised a child with brain problems. The girl that she raised got excited when the bus came. Her name was Penny. When she ran around the house, Grandma always had to calm her down.

Now that you know that heroes don't have to be the ones who jump high buildings or climb walls, you might be an awesome hero too.

Ally Claire Joan Fraser, 9

Annie Percival
(Earthly Angel)

As a little girl of eight, I remember basking in the soothing sounds of lullabies that my grandmother sang to me. I looked up, lovingly, into a face with a thousand wrinkles and kind, crystal eyes that reminded me of blue pearls on a summer's day. Annie Percival was to become a hero to me, and many others, in the quiet town of North Bay, on the north bank of Lake Nipissing.

In the 1940's, the impoverished of North Bay would come to my grandmother's back door on Jane Street, ashamed and in the dark, to beg for food. Annie, hungry herself and feeding a family, would always find something to give to these people, in terms of scraps of food, kind words, and a listening ear. Her generosity did not end there as Annie worked at the soup kitchen and then, at the age of 90, opened the North Bay Food Bank. Annie worked tirelessly at the food bank and set up a giving network system that supplies the food bank. God took Annie to heaven where she is one of his angels.

To her 16 grandchildren, she showed remarkable forward vision by recycling everything, walking everywhere, and honouring the earth. She maintained her spirit of love to us by writing us letters, making our nightgowns, and making our favorite biscuits and homemade fudge. For her stewardship and love to the North Bay people and to her grandchildren, she is truly an unsung hero.

Colleen Scanlan

Rosalie Little

YOUR BEAUTIFUL EYES

The last time I saw you, you were in a hospital bed hardly
breathing at all. Machines were going while my heart
was dropping and I thought, do I really have to say
goodbye for the last time? I wanted to look into
your beautiful eyes.

Your story on earth has just ended and mine has just begun.
On my story, you are on every page. Looking at
pictures of you makes me want to cry for in
every one of your photos, all I see is
your beautiful eyes.

I look up to the heavens knowing you're looking back down.
Now you are my guardian angel and your eyes still sparkle
like a thousand stars breaking through all the black clouds.
I know that when I miss you, all I have to do is close my
eyes, imagine you and immediately I'm looking into
your beautiful eyes.

Losing you has made me realize that even the most beautiful
things must die; the young must grow old and even the sky
must go grey. But I also know that many years from now,
when it is my turn to die, then you and I will stand together
hand in hand and once more I will be looking into
your beautiful eyes.

Mary-Rose Little, 14

Argentina Pigeau

My memére, Argentina Pigeau, is 87 years old, has 16 kids, and is just as healthy as a 60-year-old. She raised them all with Pepére, until he left when my dad was 10. She had to raise my dad and his siblings by herself, but she made it work. Six years after Pepére left, he passed away. I often think of how hard it must have been for her to lose him, twice. When he left, she still knew that he would be there if anything went wrong. He was still alive to help. When he died, she relied on herself and the eldest siblings to raise the little ones. She had to wonder if her older kids would be able to take care of the younger siblings.

If that wasn't enough, she helped to raise her grandchildren while raising her own kids. She let my family move into her house when we were moving and needed a place to stay for six months. She made dinner and made sure we were healthy and in bed on time. She made pizzas. She made them right from scratch; they were so good. We would just be waiting for them, running everywhere like we had ants in our pants. When we finally got to eat them, you wouldn't hear a word out of our stuffed mouths. In fact, Memére constantly makes sure that there is food in our hands when we are at her house, whether it is carrots or candy. She has a bowl of candy out on her table all the time. She makes great dumplings and bouillon, too.

When I was younger, she made sure everyone was happy and busy. She played 'Go Fish' with me for what seemed like hours, when everyone had gone to school or work. It just kept going. 'Go Fish' was the only game I knew, but she played it again and again for me.

She goes to every family event that she can. If Memére can't come, she'll always have a really good reason. If someone else in the family can make it but decides not to go, she'll start telling them how upset she is and that they should have been there. She'll tell them they had better be there the next time.

She lived in her house with her kids and had them sleeping in the same rooms and sharing everything. Memére had lived there for so long that when she decided it was time to move on, it was really hard to actually give it up. Memére decided to move into an independent living centre. I think she was upset at first, but later she made many friends. We were getting worried because she wasn't calling as much as usual. I guess she realized that there were more people her own age there and they liked to do the same things and they had more time to do them.

When I think of Memére, I think of her pizza, dumplings, candy, and the way she kisses me hello and good-bye. She'll make sure it is always on the lips. If your head is turned and she can't reach your lips, she'll turn your head so she gets a real kiss good-bye. Memére has done a lot in her life and has gone through so much. I've been told by some people, as a joke, that she's even repopulated the earth. She has made a huge difference in my life and I will always remember the things she does for everyone.

Samantha-Ann Boissonneault, 16

Brenda LeBlanc

My hero is my nana because of all the wonderful things that she has done for me. She's always been able to help me, no matter what she's doing. I was only five at the time and I found out that I had coagulation of the aorta and I would need a metal stint in the main aorta. They could not do open-heart surgery. My blood pressure was too high.

My operations have been simple to cope with and I recuperate well from my operations. I go to her house to get better. My surgical team is awesome and so kind. I love my grandmother a whole lot. She always knows what's wrong and helps me to feel better. So that's my story about my hero and how she's always there for me.

Molly McKenzie LeBlanc, 10

Heather Priolo

After two days of mentally replaying the past fourteen years of my life, I have come to the conclusion that the person who has affected my life in the most profound way is my grandmother, Heather, who is 66 years old.

When I was much younger, six months to four years of age, my mother would work all day. Not able to take care of myself for obvious reasons, I would spend the days at my grandmother's condo. Since my grandfather worked all day and came home for a bite to eat only at noon, I spent a lot of time around my grandmother.

The most profound materialistic objects are books; I had learned that at a very young age. Starting at 15 months, I enjoyed it when Nana would read me short, children's stories. She didn't mind reading to me; she just got annoyed when I would want her to read the same stories over and over, on the same afternoon. My love of books has carried on and, to this day, I can't help but think that the repetitive story-reading is the foundation of that love.

Due to the fact that my grandmother lived at home all day, she did all the cleaning. I suppose that influenced me at such an early age. I became fascinated with brooms, vacuums, and cleaning products. It was such an odd fixation that, when shopping at a grocery store, I would scamper down the aisles, blurting out the names of all the cleaning products on the shelves. The employees and shoppers at the store were bewildered that a one-year-old could read so well. The reality of it all was that I had memorized the products, due to extensive examinations of flyers with Nana at my side.

Visiting my grandmother wasn't always the most enjoyable time for me, though. One afternoon, my father stopped in to pick me up. As my grandmother was socializing with him, I scurried into the kitchen, opened the cupboard, retrieved the cooking oil, ran into the living room and dumped it on the carpet. With that, my dad swooped over to me and put me in my crib, located in the spare room. I moaned for my grandmother, shocked that she would leave me in my crib while she got to have all the fun, cleaning. I now realize that she did that to teach me discipline and I never spilled cooking oil on a carpet again!

Nana can be light-hearted, too, and doesn't always get mad, like when I had orange pop in my cheeks and she smacked them, thinking they were filled with air. She just laughed and cleaned up the mess.

I know sometimes I get mad when she tells me to do something, homework-related or not. I've learned to respect her opinion, as well as the opinions of other people. My grandmother has taught me so much and has made me a better person.

Tyler Mason, 14

Mary Flemming

My hero is my grandma because she takes me shopping and loves me. She takes me to school every day so that I don't have to take the bus. She takes me to her house to sleep overnight. My grandma has black and grey hair. She likes to go paddling in the summer and she belongs to The Warriors of Hope. She works at Kennedy's Insurance. She comes from Prince Edward Island.

Caitlin Howard, 8

Melvina Novack
(Doing Good on Earth)

At 22 years of age, I had the wonderful luck of going through open-heart surgery. Of course, after such a traumatic procedure, I had to be taken care of in all aspects of life... literally. My grandmother, a woman from the small township of Calvin, came to my rescue when I needed help the most. She took four months out of her life to stay with me in the big city of Toronto, a place of pure anxiety for her because it was such a different way of life. The volume of people, the aggressive drivers, and overall lifestyle made her fearful, but she overcame her fear in order to help with my recovery. She was very brave to come to my aid for such a long period of time.

She did everything for me and I mean everything. She helped me bathe, she cooked my food, she cleaned my house, she took care of my pets, she reassured me when complications arose, and she escorted me everywhere. She walked with me because I was limited in my mobility, she massaged my excruciatingly sore muscles when I could barely move, she talked on the phone for me when I couldn't catch my breath, and she loved and cared for me. These selfless examples exemplified the true goodness in her.

Melvina Novack, the name given to my Mémère at birth, was a devout Catholic who always tried to embrace the teaching of St. Therese, which is to imitate God's love by doing good on earth. She accomplished this, not only by helping me through recovery after the surgery, but by completing the exact same tasks, again, for my brother, only one year later (yeah, he had that wonderful luck, as well). Her ability to put her family first has always inspired me to imitate her love by doing good towards others. She was truly great.

Unfortunately, Mémère lost her battle with cancer on September 24, 2006. My grandmother was my life. She was my best friend, my confidant, and my second mother.

Tracy Sloan

CHAPTER NINE

OUR GRANDFATHERS

What a bargain grandchildren are! I give them my loose change, and they give me a million dollars worth of pleasure.

Gene Perret

Walter Walker

Some people say that you can tell a person's past and what they have been through by their appearance and their actions in everyday life. Can you truly recognize what a person has gone through just by those characteristics?

Today, if you saw Walter Walker, you would see an 87-year-old man, his memory slowly passing away along with his life. You would see the sadness in his eyes from the lonely days that await him in his hospital bed; but if you really knew him, you would be able to see so much more.

When I see Walter Walker, I do not see just another mature person on this planet who is taking life's natural course. I see a loving great-grandfather and father to six children. I see a man who fought for his country in World War II and then started a dairy farm so that he could give his family a good life. He has been through cancer once already, the result of which included losing his eye. Every time I would go to see him at his house in the little township of Eau Claire, I would never hear him complain about his poor vision or his loss of hearing that were definite effects of old age.

When I see Walter Walker, I see a man whose love for music will always remain with him. In his life he has made a total of over 30 violins, by hand. If you have ever even looked at a violin, you would see how much time and patience it takes for something so small to be created, to make such a beautiful sound. We used to play together when I knew only one song; he was always teaching me new things, and when he was too sick and sore to play, he would sit in his chair and listen to me play for him. There would be no words said, but his smile said a thousand.

In his last years at home, he made one last violin before he went to the hospital in Mattawa, where he is today. This violin was made from the hands of a frail man who took more care and time than ever to make this beautiful instrument. The effects of his age did not show on this violin. It looked magnificent! He gave that violin to me. I was almost afraid to play it because of the amount of care and love that was used to make it.

Walter Walker taught me that music isn't just what you read on paper. It is what comes out of your heart and is played from your soul, to make something that is a great gift from God. I look up to him because of everything that he has accomplished in life and everything that he has taught people. He is my great-grandfather and my friend.

Jenny Kuehni, 14

Ronald McIntyre

When I was younger, I would try to do everything I could with my poppa. He was the only predominant father-figure in my life. My poppa was a big man. He was 6' 4" tall and weighed about 240 pounds. At his heaviest, he was almost 300 pounds.

When I turned four, I loved to play hide-and-go-seek with my sister. My favorite hiding place was to run over to my poppa, who would be on the couch watching the Toronto Blue Jays or having a nap, and climb up and hide under the blanket he always had. Every night the Blue Jays' game was on, I ran downstairs when we had to leave, knowing if I made it to my poppa that I would be able to stay another 10 minutes, so I could watch a bit of the game.

My poppa worked for Ontario Northland. He was an engineer, so he drove the trains. One of my fondest memories is when my poppa and I went to the train on the waterfront; my poppa knew the man who drove it because they used to work together. I got to sit at the front, wear the man's engineer hat, and drive the train. That sounds really fun, and it was, but all I got to do was blow the horn and occasionally pull a lever. It may sound boring, but it's the thought that counts and it was a great thought. I loved to spend time with my poppa. He had train puzzles, train models, and lots of train hats. I loved trains when I was little because it was something that my poppa and I shared.

Another interest that I shared with my poppa was fishing. I remember the first time I went fishing with my poppa, I was six, and it is another great memory I will carry with me throughout my life. My poppa, Pastor Gerry, the reverend of our church, and I went fishing. We took our little blue boat which still sits on the beach at my nan's house. I don't know why or where we stopped, but always after a short trip, we would stop and my poppa would say, "This is the spot". I never knew why it was the spot or how my poppa knew, but we always seemed to catch fish. We were out for two hours and I caught two fish; well, technically, only one because I traded for the other one. As we were fishing, a man in a boat came up and asked if he could have some worms because he had used all of his and my poppa said, "Ask Stephen. They're his worms," because I had taken my allowance and bought the worms the day before we went. I gave the man some worms and he decided to give us one of the fish he had caught. I remember this well because he threw us a medium-sized pickerel and I went to catch it. When I caught it, it slipped out of my hand, but my poppa, showing amazing agility for a man of his age, reached out and caught the fish in midair.

The other fish that I caught was a pike that, to me, was incredibly huge; it was nearly as big as I was, but when we brought it home, my poppa said we couldn't eat it because he didn't filet pikes. I was crestfallen by not being able to keep my trophy, but we gave it to a couple at our church that made some delicious soup from it (and I know it was delicious because they sent us a bowl). I still have the pictures and the fond memories of that great day that I went fishing with my poppa.

Stephen Fleury, 15

George Edgerton
(A Little Bit of Life)

I remember it like a hazy dream. Light was shining all around; I could feel the sunlight touching my heart and warming my body. I opened my eyes and walked down the old, creaky stairs. At the bottom, I passed the old-fashioned dishwasher where my grandma would lay a new batch of homemade cookies each time I visited.

My grandpa used to wake up early each morning when the birds first began to sing. He would eat a bowl of Shredded Wheat and half of a grapefruit. I woke before him on this morning. He slept for an extra few minutes. I prepared the breakfast; I didn't eat until he joined me. He was surprised to see me so early and gave me a warm hug. When we were done our cereal, he cut the grapefruit and we shared it. It seemed to give him a little extra life each morning. When we were done, we sat and talked; I'm not sure about what, but it was probably dinosaurs and other little secrets that seemed so important to me at the time. When the others awoke, they laughed at the sight of us - two generations sitting apart and enjoying ourselves.

My grandfather died seven years ago and my grandmother moved to the apartment building behind the old house. We still go and visit, but I haven't had any Shredded Wheat in awhile.

Tom Sapinski, 1993

Dennis Molloy

While driving down the main street in Balmertown, a small, gold-mining town in Northern Ontario, you will pass the Dennis Molloy Fire Station. You might then ask yourself, who was Dennis Molloy? He was my grandpa.

My grandpa was a miner at the Placer Dome Campbell Mine and he was the Fire Chief for the Township of Golden. At least two times a year, my grandpa and grandma would drive three days to come to North Bay. Even though he was a very busy man, my grandpa always had time for our family. He would take time off his jobs to bring my family and me to the cottage or come to my house and spend time with us.

Almost every Christmas since I was born, my grandpa and grandma would come to North Bay and spend the holidays with my family. My grandpa had been diagnosed with colon cancer, but was still able to visit us even though he was often not feeling well. In December 1999, my grandma and grandpa came to visit for a week. We knew, in our hearts, that this might be his last Christmas with us because his health was beginning to decline. The day after my grandparents arrived in North Bay, my mom had to call an ambulance because my grandpa was having trouble breathing. Little did we know that he would never again return to our house.

One of my most vivid memories of this visit was waking up on Christmas morning and not having my grandpa there to enjoy Christmas Day with my family. I remember taking

Christmas presents from underneath the tree, but being unable to pass them to my grandpa to watch him open them. He never did get to open his gifts that year.

When I woke up on January 4, 2000, my mom told me that my grandpa had died. Everyone at my house was very sad, but I was only six years old at the time and I didn't really understand what had actually happened. His funeral was held in Balmertown. My dad carried my grandpa's ashes on the plane. My mom told me that, at his funeral, there were hundreds of people. The funeral had to be held at the Recreation Centre because there weren't any other halls big enough for all the people that they knew would attend. As my family left the hall where my grandpa's funeral was held, all of the firemen that worked with, and knew, my grandpa were lined up outside the door, saluting as our family passed by.

Thinking back on it now, I realize that even though my grandpa had cancer and two jobs, he still had time to bring me and my sister to the cottage, drive our family to Winnipeg in the summer, bring me fishing, and to visit North Bay as often as he could. I will always remember my grandpa for the many special times we had together.

I can tell how important my grandpa was in his community from the stories I've heard from people who knew him and the fact that the fire station was named after him. He always put his family first. He was my grandpa.

Carly Collins

Edward Toner

Growing up, I spent a lot of time with Grandpa. I remember waking up in the morning with a 10-dollar bill by my bedside and the smell of bacon and home fries. We did many things, from mowing the lawn to working in the shop. Even though I never really did anything in the shop, I watched and learned. One special activity I looked forward to the most was putting on his cowboy boots and hat. He used to tell me stories about cowboys and draw pictures.

He lived just outside of the city, about a 20-minute drive. If I wanted a movie or even to just go to the candy store, he would never hesitate to drive me in for something I wanted. If something personal came up in his life and he had no one else to talk to, he could always talk to me. I felt the same way about him. I can't say I was his favorite grandchild, but I felt that we had a special bond.

I was at home one weekend and my mom walked into the room and said, "I just got off the phone with Grandma. Grandpa is in the hospital." This was devastating news. When we got to the hospital, they explained that he had pneumonia and that things did not look good. His hands and feet were blue, and he was having a lot of trouble talking. I never doubted for one minute that he would walk out of that hospital because I knew he was a strong person. It was only about a week later and he was back at home.

The following year, around Christmas, he got very sick again, but he hated the hospital and he refused to go back. Grandma took care of him and nursed him. Everyone thought he had pneumonia. His symptoms worsened and they finally had to call an ambulance. At the hospital, they had to put him in isolation because they said he could have tuberculosis in his lungs, which is highly-contagious and deadly. I was told to put on a gown and a mask. As I went in, I almost broke into tears, but I held my composure because I knew my grandpa wouldn't like to see me sad. He grabbed my hand and he was trying to talk to me, but I had no idea what he was saying. At this stage, he had almost completely lost his memory. I'm not sure if anyone else heard him, but I heard him say my name and he kept on trying to talk to me. I felt so bad that I could not understand him, so I nodded my head and tried to make out the words he was saying. The doctors came in and told us we had to leave the room. I didn't even get to say goodbye. The next day, my mom came over to my dad's house and she gave us the news. He had passed early in the morning, in his sleep.

I sat through all of the speeches at the funeral and talked to the relatives about their stories about him. At the end, I placed my hand on the casket to say my final goodbye and that was the only true time I burst into tears. I could not stop. My family and friends comforted me. His spirit still lives on today.

Billy Spilchuk, 15

Jacob Raymond Prediger

Ever since I can remember, I have spent every possible holiday and weekend at my grandparents' house, or at least I had until the Christmas of 2001, when we spent the weekend before the Christmas holidays started. I was in my preteens and starting to get an attitude. I was bratty and sarcastic and, like any other kid, I was annoyed at my grandparents for trying to tell me what to do.

The following Tuesday, we were called early in the morning while I was getting ready for school. On Monday night or early Tuesday morning, my Papa passed away in his sleep. At that moment, I hadn't really understood the situation but I cried over what my mother said when it sunk in for her. Sobbing in my father's arms, she managed to say, "I don't have a daddy anymore ..."

On the morning of the wake, I dreamt of the sound of Papa's stomping feet coming to get me up and active and outside. I got out of bed excited, thinking the last few days had all been a sick dream, but after seeing the faces of my family as they were eating breakfast, I knew it wasn't the last few days that had been the sick dream, but the one I was having.

The strain of the situation hadn't hit me until the middle of his wake. The paramedics had waited until we got there to take his body away and I saw him, quiet and cold, on the couch. Everything seemed fuzzy, like a dream. At the wake, everything became so real and vivid. Everyone around me was reminiscing and would go on about something that I didn't know about him. When the shock wore off, I realized that I had been acting so stupid, and that was just before he died. I felt that his last thoughts of me must have been, "what a nasty kid to be like that," and that is when I went to him and said, "I'm sorry, Papa. I am. I love you, even if I acted like I don't like you." Then, when I touched his cold face, it seemed so wrong that I couldn't see his happy-go-lucky grin. I realized fully and completely that I would never be able to say that to him. At the time, I felt that he never knew that I truly loved him. I was so upset that I wasn't able to go to his funeral reception.

That day, I promised that I would never act that way again and that I would treat everyone with the respect and care they deserve. I promised that if I ever cared about someone, I would say so every time I said good-bye so that if anything happened, I would not regret anything. This was also the end of my attitude problem.

This isn't the only reason why I admire him. I believe that he is the only person I know who did everything he wanted, even if he was risking his life. He died with no regrets and the more I talk to older people, the more I find out how hard it is not having regrets. I suppose that I admire him just because of everything he was, all the great things he did, and how he helped make me the person I am today, without even knowing it.

Jessica Dahl, 16

Alexander M. Davidson

As a youngster with a great passion for painting, I eagerly anticipated any trip my family would take to see my grandparents in Winnipeg, Manitoba. My grandfather, Alexander M. Davidson, was a quiet man who, besides working in the newspaper-publishing business as owner of the Norwood Press, was an outstanding artist, painting both watercolours and oils. He was my hero. I admired his paintings and I have five of his original paintings hanging in my art gallery. He passed away in 1956 and I have, in my possession, the last painting he was working on.

In the summer of 1947, I was visiting him in Winnipeg and went down to the Hudson's Bay Store and brought back a watercolour painting kit, containing numerous colours. I hurried back to his place to show him my great purchase. He looked at the many colours on the tray and said in a quiet, but stern, manner, "Take that back to the store and bring back the three primary colours - red, yellow and blue, and learn how to mix paint."

Today, after professionally producing paintings for over 40 years, I have never forgotten him telling me what I consider to be the best art lesson I have ever had in my life.

Jack Lockhart

Norman White

I look up to my granddad for his positive outlook on life and his hard work ethic. His life revolves around helping others and making them feel good. He's a great laugh and can always pick me up when I'm down. What I didn't know was to what extent he actually went to keep others happy and healthy.

Norman White, a veteran of World War II, grew up in a family of eight children in a coal-mining community in South Wales. From a young age, he sometimes saw tragedy in the mines and learned the value of sharing and doing unto others as you wish they would do unto you. He then went on to care for two sons, four grandchildren, and two great-grandchildren, never once losing his spark for life.

While taking care of his wife, who was terribly ill, he always put himself last. Hiding his fear of losing his wife, he helped prevent her from becoming afraid. There was something else he was hiding, though. In 1999, Grandpa was diagnosed with bladder cancer, but kept it a secret from the rest of the family to protect them. He stayed by his wife's side, speeding down to the hospital for his treatments and rushing back so as not to waste a minute of precious time that could be spent with his wife. He did everything she could not do, such as buying groceries, cooking, and cleaning, as well as doing the handiwork and filling the traditional role of man of the house. He was in constant agony, but wouldn't dare put himself first because that would mean that others would have to wait to be taken care of.

He battled his way through the cancer and continued to look after the love of his life while keeping a positive attitude. He welcomes us into his home with a warm heart and often spends time sending letters and cards overseas. He is 80 now, but he has the spirit of an 18-year-old and continues to inspire everyone and anyone he meets.

Bethan White

Herb Brown
(Thank You to a Model Citizen)

Gazing out over the stark, frozen vastness of Lake Nipissing, Herb Brown reminisces about a life of service to the community that he loves.

"North Bay was a wonderful place to grow up. Even though my father died when I was only five years old, my mother always made sure that I was involved in all of the activities available in a small town. I was brought up in a traditional Jewish home. I was fortunate to live in a community like North Bay where I was able to play basketball on an Anglican Church team. I also attended public school and made many friends, including those who belonged to a variety of different religious institutions."

Mr. Brown went on to describe life as the smallest and youngest student at North Bay Collegiate Institute and Vocational School. It was also during this time that he was chosen to type the story of the Dionne Quintuplets' first birthday for a CBC documentary. For a 14-year-old high school student, taking part in documenting an international story was quite an experience.

"One of my first jobs was with Marvin Hockman, an old-fashioned entrepreneur who taught me everything I needed to know about the auto-parts business. Armed with this knowledge, when the Second World War broke out, I was one of the lucky ones who was needed more at home than on the front. I took basic training and I was stationed at the

Parts Ordinance Centre in Ottawa, for the duration of the conflict. It was also during that time that I met the love of my life, Geetie Litwack, who has been at my side ever since."

It was then that Mrs. Brown entered the room with a tray of homemade strudel and other delicacies. I soon understood why it was that this marriage had endured the test of time.

Over the years, he has been instrumental in the development of many facilities in the area. He speaks with pride of the part he played in bringing a university to North Bay and being chairman of a local hospital during a difficult period of transition.

"I was President of the Chamber of Commerce at the time and also Chair of the School of Nursing. I was named chairman of a committee formed to convince the Ontario government to establish a university in North Bay. At that time, several of us traveled to Toronto to attempt to persuade the government of the day that North Bay would be the best location for such an institution. Unfortunately, it was not meant to be and Laurentian University was given the go-ahead."

Mr. Brown and the other community leaders involved did not give up. A partnership was formed which included an affiliate college of Laurentian University, a group wishing to form a community college, the School of Nursing, and the North Bay Normal School. Some part-time classes commenced in 1962 at the old Casselhome facility. Years of hard work eventually paid off and, in 1993, Nipissing University received its charter.

Mr. Brown served as Chairman of the Board of Nipissing

University College during the formative years. He also somehow found time to chair several other organizations, including the North Bay Rotary Club. He was also named President of the Sons of Jacob Synagogue, an organization which he has chaired for approximately 30 years. His community involvement has also included chairmanship of the North Bay and District Cancer Society and St. Joseph's Hospital.

For his efforts, Herb Brown has received numerous awards. Laurentian University awarded Mr. Brown an Honourary Doctorate of Law so that he may now be properly addressed as Dr. Brown. His business colleagues recognized Herb Brown as Automotive Parts Jobber of the year during the 1980's and, during the same period, the Kiwanis Club of North Bay named him North Bay's Citizen of the Year, the first person to be so recognized.

"I have always been embarassed by any public recognition I have received," he says, "But of all the accomplishments I have been involved with, I am proudest to be a part of establishing a university in North Bay. I don't believe they will ever make a movie about my life, but if they did I would choose Tom Cruise for the lead character. My favourite role in life has been as father and grandfather to a wonderful family."

Talia Brown

Regis Young

There is a very special person who has impacted my life in so many ways. He is my grandfather, Regis Young, or if you know him on a personal note, Saint Regis.

Grandpa had a very hard life. Born in Hunters Point, the adventure began. The middle-child of a family of nine, six boys and three girls, my grandfather worked hard to accomplish the goal his family had set for him: school. Although not very common among many Native Americans, my grandfather stayed in school up until the sixth grade when he was forced to leave to begin his working life. He would work at a tourist camp for one dollar a day to provide school books for his brothers and sisters. Not only did he go to work every day but he was forced to walk there, being a part of an underprivileged family.

At the tender age of 17, my grandfather met his best friend and soul mate, Sonia McLaughlin, from another Native American family. They were 'meant to be' from the start. If you asked him who his rock was, he would be sure to say his family first, of course, but mainly his wife. My grandfather is unlike any other. He worked for almost nothing and gave his everything, every day.

My mother and her two brothers grew up in a house that many would have found uncomfortable. They shared a bedroom, but my grandfather would think only that it brought them closer. My grandfather faced a challenge with his stuttering. He has a speech impediment that has been with him since birth. Some may not understand him, but I get every joke he makes, even when they are directed at me.

Nothing holds my grandfather back. He comes to every one of my brother's home hockey games, every special event I am in, and even just comes down to visit. He is a very family-oriented man. My brothers and I are all eager for old age, just so we can be like him. When my nanny Sonia goes out of town on business, my grandfather is there by her side to keep her company and to split the drive. On one special occasion, I was lucky enough to accompany them on a trip to Montreal. My grandmother was there for work and my grandfather proved to be my best friend. We spent a day in the sun, shopping, laughing, and just enjoying each other's company. That was a weekend I will never forget.

My grandfather, just this year, overcame a very difficult obstacle - death. He had unusual pain in his chest. It brought us to tears when we were forced to send him in an ambulance to the hospital. Despite his strong passion for life, we saw only the worst in his weak eyes. It was at this time that I reminisced about all the pain and pleasure I had gone through with him. Not only did I see his life, but I saw my own life flash before my eyes. Seeing him so weak, unable to be himself, I feared the worst. Witnessing him lying there for the first time in my life, I really felt as though I had lost him when he spoke clearly, without a stumble or stutter in his words. I did not know when my last words to him would be, or if they would even be able to stumble out of my mouth. I wondered what to say. Should I say goodbye? Would that mean that we had accepted defeat? All I knew was that, at that very moment, he was my hero. I understood the pain he went through to get to where he was, to get me to where I am. Without him, there would be no me. Now I faced the same predicament. I could not bear to lose someone so close, so great. I could not, and I would not, lose my grandfather.

For the next two weeks, I ate, slept, and dreamt only of my grandfather in the hospital. I, not being a religious church-goer, made amends with God. I asked Him if I could have just one thing: could my grandfather stay here with us, just for a little while longer. I couldn't bear to lose him at such a young age, with so much more for us to do together. I repeated to myself, "He is going to be okay. He is going to make it. God won't let me down. God won't let us down...He can't...He just can't." It was at the end of those two long, hard weeks that my prayer was finally answered. We did not have a celebration in answer of his return; instead we had light hearts. We were grateful to have him back, even though he was not at full-strength.

It was explained to us at a young age that to live, you must die. It is a cycle. My grandfather showed me just how precious life is.

Brittany Roy, 13

Eugene Spilchuk

For too long he hid the fact that he had a golf ball-sized lump on his body. When he finally went to the doctor to have it checked out, he accepted the grim news and said he would enjoy playing cribbage with his relatives in heaven. But as the months went on and he started going for chemotherapy treatments, things were looking a bit better and he began carrying his comb in his back pocket, even though he had lost all his hair from the chemo.

My grandfather, Eugene Spilchuk, who my brother, sister, and cousins call Bachee, had a very successful business career being 'Gene the Handyman' and then being part-owner of Seymour Windows. He and my grandmother, Joyce, recently built their dream home on the escarpment in North Bay. When Bachee was diagnosed with cancer, they decided to sell the house because it would be too big and too much for grandma to take care of, if he were to pass away. Still, this did not get his spirits down. He continued to go for his chemo treatments and, today, has made a full recovery.

Bachee beat cancer and has inspired me to never give up hope, even if situations sometimes appear bleak. He taught me that no one should ever let anything get their spirits down, not even a horrible disease like cancer.

Mike Spilchuk, 16

CHAPTER TEN

OUR
CELEBRATED
HEROES

*Dignity does not come in possessing
honours, but in deserving them.*

Aristotle

Jesus Christ

When I was a young boy, every once in a while, my parents, being good Scottish Presbyterians, would go to church on Sunday. They weren't particularly religious, just the "once in a while" kind of congregants. You know, Christmas, Easter, that sort of thing; and I'm sure my father went along just to please my mother. As infrequent as it was, whenever they did go, I would unavoidably go with them. Once at the church, they would quarantine me in a big room with a horde of unfamiliar children, whose parents were evidently just as callous, and then make what can only be described as a "great escape". This, I soon learned, was called "Sunday School". I hated it. I would weep unbearably every time, grasping in vain at my parents as they fled the room. One particular Sunday, I threw enough of a tantrum that they summoned my parents to take away their unruly child. So that Sunday, my parents brought me into the chapel with them for the first time.

The inside of the chapel was pleasant, but modest. If you've never been inside a Presbyterian church before, they are typically unassuming and unpretentious, as are most Presbyterians. St. Paul's was no exception. Nothing too fancy; wood paneled walls, a few coloured windows with people painted on them, and a table covered with a purple tablecloth where a nice old bearded man, with glasses and dressed in black, passed out little bits of bread and grape juice for us to snack on during the service. There were, of course, the obligatory wooden pews, complete with little round holes in the back to put the tiny little cups in when you had finished your juice. Most prominently, in the center of the back wall, was a very large, wooden cross. There was no scantily clad, dying man nailed to it, just a big, wooden cross. We stood up and sang a little, sat down, closed our eyes while the old bearded man talked, stood up, sang a little more, sat down, stood up, sat again. Then the nice bearded man with the glasses stood at a podium and talked for what seemed a really long time, once in a while pausing to read aloud from a little black book. Clinging to my mother's side in the pew, I sat quietly as he spoke. Being a mere five- or six-year-old, I was, of course, far too young to comprehend what the old man went on about. Yet, as I listened, I was drawn to the big cross on the wall. Then, not suddenly, but as quietly as I sat there staring at that big old cross, it struck me that whatever that thing meant, it was "the truth". I didn't know exactly what it was that it stood for. Yet, even then, at five or six, I "knew that I knew that I knew" that whatever it was, it was "The Truth".

Since that Sunday, over the past thirty-odd years or so, I have come to understand more fully what exactly it is that that big old cross stands for. But even as my comprehension has increased over time, it cannot be stated more plainly than it was that Sunday morning. It is still simply "The Truth". To be more precise - not it, but the one with whom it has become most associated, is "The Truth". Jesus said, "I am the Way, the Truth and the Life."

We, in the 21st century, have been conditioned to the idea that personal taste and choice is a sort of birthright. Indeed, we are burdened in every area with an overabundance of choice, not the least of which is an overabundance of choice in the theological arena. From Taoism to Hinduism, Judaism to Zoroastrianism, from monasticism to even space aliens, how does one know which is "The Truth", when they all claim to be such? Like having too many channels on the T.V to choose from, we click around looking for something that catches our interest until we eventually conclude there's nothing good on and then just turn it off. That is what many have done with regards to issues of faith; just turned it off. Too much choice has led to no choice, leaving people declaring, "Ah, it's all the same anyway."

Yet, may I propose that, among the pantheon of gods and demagogues that one has to choose from, the story of the carpenter from Nazareth stands quite unique as the greatest example of love the world has ever witnessed. This story of Love (God) creating the universe and having his very creation used against him in order to demonstrate love, through the ultimate sacrifice of love, is quite simply the most profound thing that I have ever heard. Add to this, that creation was designed towards this purpose from the very beginning, and it becomes even more overwhelming. Paradoxically, the story of Jesus, as God in the flesh, is simultaneously the source of mankind's ultimate rebellion against God and our ultimate redemption. As I remember back to that big old cross on the wall, I now understand that it truly is the "greatest story ever told".

Lloyd McMillan

Lynn Johnston

From the outside looking in, our workplace is a diverse, unique team of colleagues and probably not your typical local working group. Our grand total of five women is a mixture of first and second generations of British, French, Ukrainian, Russian and Dutch nationalities. Collectively, we converse in five languages, we are in our 20s, 30s, 40s and 50s, and we have differing viewpoints on politics, religion, fashion, music, entertainment and relationships. We have, call it fate if you like, somehow been united together to work as a team for reasons that are greater than we are. None of us filled out a job application for our current positions. None of us were even looking for work at the time. There is an expression that speaks to water always finding the easiest path to its destination - we just "go with the flow." Who determines "the flow"?

Lynn Johnston has impacted many, many citizens around the world. Our story isn't public relations rhetoric; we work closely with Lynn and have witnessed the genuine woman behind the pen and ink. With close to thirty years of recounting the lives of the Patterson family, in her syndicated work of "For Better or For Worse," chances are she has recounted a scenario, or two, from your own family history. Readers often wonder if Lynn has planted informants or recording devices into their homes! It is because she is genuine and empathetic that people relate to her so easily.

Lynn introduced the world to Mr. Lawrence Poirier. Lawrence is an entrepreneur in the landscaping sector, he has post-secondary education, he's an only child to his divorced mom, his mom is white, his dad is Latino, and he's in a healthy relationship with his partner Nicholas. Today, even with his many stigmas, Lawrence could be someone each of us knows; but close to 15 years ago when he appeared in the strip as a gay man, he was a stranger. Solely on the fact of his being gay, the public closed doors on him; solely on the fact of his being gay, the public also found strength to paddle into uncharted waters. Unbeknownst to Lynn, she was doing her part in changing the flow that people follow.

The numbers "nine" and "eleven" will forever be linked to the events of September 11th, 2001. Core human values of faith, hope and charity were wrenched and challenged. One year later, as the globe was still wrestling for normalcy, readers of "For Better or For Worse" joined Elizabeth Patterson's daily routine of dining in her university cafeteria with her friends. The comic joked how Elizabeth was watching her waist line as she ordered a tossed salad, yet she nibbled on the French fries of her pals. Pretty everyday stuff, or so we thought. The volume of snail mail, email, online discussion group messages, and media requests for interviews on account of this strip was astounding! With the world still trying to figure out what to do with itself, could so many people be paying attention to Liz's weight? No. It had to do with Lynn illustrating a typical university cafeteria setting, including a Muslim student wearing her hijab, just as she would have on September 10th, 2001. The flow changed again.

Upon graduation from university, Liz Patterson ventured into her career as a teacher and accepted a position in the fictitious Northern Ontario community of Mtigwaki. With help from her friends and her natural sense of curiosity, Lynn shared the culture and traditions of First Nations people. Cedar boughs, fancy dancers, eagle feathers and pow-wows may not necessarily be part of your everyday, but they are an important part of someone's everyday. Because of her empathy with Canada's First Nations people, Lynn was able to introduce millions of readers to their way of life. Again, our team of five was impressed by the momentum of the public interest in First Nations life, its fascination and willingness to flow into more unexplored waters.

April Patterson has entered high school and has also entered the palm-sweating realm of peer pressure, fashion critiques and fitting in - sooner, rather than later. So has Shannon Lake, April's newfound friend. A difference between the two young ladies is that Shannon has special needs. Her learning curve bends in a different direction than April's. Shannon joined the Patterson cast in "For Better or For Worse" with the blessing of Lynn's niece, Stephanie, who has special needs of her own. Since the launch of this new dynamic character in Lynn's comic, the challenges and victories of those with special needs have been celebrated beyond simply the page of newsprint. Stephanie has adopted an online following of people curious about those with special needs. Her reach has been further stretched into Canada and the U.S., with public speaking engagements on the topic of inclusion of people with disabilities. The character of Shannon Lake has opened up yet another body of water for us to flow into.

For Lynn, her gift of creative illustration and writing has been a vehicle for expressing her empathy. As much as she works in an entertainment medium, her storylines and illustrations have spoken to a global audience. Take away all of the public attention from her comic strip, take away her pen and ink, and you'll find a woman who promotes and fosters cultural diversity, social responsibility and global acceptance. She is not afraid to ask questions in an attempt to truly understand those around her. In doing so, she has broken, and will continue to break, ground for the waters to flow and others to follow. With much love and admiration,

Liuba Liamzina
Laura Piche
Allison Zadorozny
Jackie Levesque
Stephanie VanDoleweerd

Christine Fortin

I see her every Tuesday, from 7:25-8:10, and have been for five years. She is a caring, brave, and happy person who is always busy! Christine Fortin is my piano teacher.

Christine has gone through a lot in her life. Her son, Patrick, died of AIDS at a young age. He was a hemophiliac who was given a blood transfusion with tainted blood. The effect that something like that must have on a person is unimaginable to me. It would be immensely difficult to get over and move on.

Christine and her husband continue to work towards Patrick's dream of finding a cure for AIDS. Patrick 4 Life is a program run by the Fortin's, in memory of Patrick. It is dedicated to raising money for AIDS research and awareness. Christine has also presented many speeches about her son and the effect his life, and loss, has had on her and the family. It takes a lot of courage to be able to talk about something like that, but it doesn't matter to Christine because she wants so much to make a difference. It's inspiring that someone who has lost and gone through an ordeal can overcome and help prevent other families from experiencing the same pain.

On top of all this, Christine still finds the time to teach her 80 piano students every week! Her enthusiasm and appreciation of music is obvious during the piano lesson. When I switched to Christine from a different piano teacher, I was welcomed whole-heartedly and was soon advancing in piano faster than ever. Her teaching techniques make piano more fun and less work. She always has a smile on her face and is patient when you struggle with something new. Most of all, she puts her teaching ahead of all the other things she is busy with. By doing this, she teaches her students something more important than any musical trick or theory: true commitment to the things you love.

Christine's love of life has taught me to treasure every day that I have and to not take anything for granted. She has inspired me in my music and has shown me that I can accomplish anything if I truly want it. Her personality and inner strength shine in a way that make you want to be a better person.

Meghan Robidoux

Dion Phaneuf

I play hockey. I love hockey and hockey is everything to me. My favourite number is three. My position is defense and the only person I want to be, when I'm older, is Dion Phaneuf. He is number three and plays defense for the Calgary Flames NHL hockey team. He led the league last year in defenseman goals and for most hits as a rookie.

Dion Phaneuf is amazing. He skates well and has a bomb of a slap shot and a rocket wrist shot. He has amazing patience with the puck, sees the ice well, and makes great plays and, best of all, he hits like a freight train. He had a lot of knock-out hits last year.

I have never met him and I don't know where he played before the NHL, but I do know that he is the hockey player that I idolize, the kind of person I want to be; he has the type of life that I want to have. Even before Dion started playing hockey in Calgary, I wanted to go there for school or even for vacation. It attracted me because of the great hockey opportunities there and the mountains to bike on.

To sum it up and to make it simple, I don't want to be Dion Phaneuf, but I want to be in his situation. I want to be Ryan Burton with that life and I will do anything I have to in order to give myself the opportunity to get to where he is today.

Ryan Burton, 14

The Quiet Cowboy

Have you ever met a person who seemed the most unlikely to become famous and yet, you feel so good when they do? It was in the early 1960's and I was working that winter at Mike's Supermarket in Timmins, mostly at the lunch counter. One morning he was there, a very quiet gentleman wearing a black cowboy hat, black shirt and black pants, looking like a cowboy. He sat there with a seven-cent cup of coffee. He was very pale and skinny.

The next morning, he appeared again and I found out his name was Tom; still only a cup of coffee. So on the third morning, I asked, "Are you hungry, Tom?" I have been known for my soft touch, so I slipped him a pair of day-old doughnuts we were not supposed to sell anymore. Tom devoured them in a hurry. I found out he was hitchhiking across Canada. Later on, I slipped him some day-old sandwiches. All winter long, he was my first seven-cent, coffee-only customer. He was always very polite, saying, "Yes, ma'am," "No, ma'am," "Thank you, ma'am." I really started to like him and I found out that he sang for his supper and a room in the hotel across the street. He invited the girls from Mike's Supermarket to come and listen to him sing and play his guitar.

So, on our first Wednesday afternoon off, we got a table and ordered our 15-cent glass of draft beer. We were a little surprised when he started to sing and, on a piece of plywood, he was stomping his feet to the rhythm of the songs that he had written himself. He made up songs about us girls from the supermarket. I wish I had written them down; they were very cute and personal.

Another member of the part-time staff of Mike's was a rather debonair French man who was also named Tom. He sang and played guitar One Tom sat at one end of the long counter and the other Tom sat as far away as possible, on the other side. Our French Tom, with his black wavy hair and moustache, was quite the ladies man, dressed for the office. One day, when I was alone with him, he told me, "You know your friend, Tom, the Stomper? Well, he thinks he can sing so well, he wants to make records. He wants to become famous. The poor guy can't sing worth diddle. He'll get nowhere." Famous last words.

I found out Tom's last name was Connors. That winter, we saved thin grocery cartons. Tom had made himself some tapes and sent them in homemade cartons to the radio station. About a year later, some gentlemen discovered Tom. He began to sing in a much classier bar and people really started to like him. He was finally getting paid and could come and buy a hamburger, with the works, and leave a generous tip. He was still the likeable, quiet fellow.

For a few years after I moved to North Bay, I did not hear much about Tom until the tapes started to appear in the music stores. I would play them and tell my friends, "I know this fellow, you know." Many years later when he got the order of Canada, I wish I could have sat beside the French Tom and asked him how his musical career was going. I don't think he ever sold a record.

In early 2000, while I was a volunteer at our Capitol Centre, I heard Stompin' Tom was coming. Every Stompin' Tom fan in Northern Ontario was there. When he came out on the stage, it seemed as if I was looking at the same fellow I knew 40 years ago, only his clothes were a bit more expensive.

I went to sit in the very last row near the wall, reserved for the volunteers, when a tall, handsome stranger came and sat beside me. A few minutes later he said, "Hi, Margie, how are you?" I whispered, "Fine." I did not know that guy. He had read my nametag. When the lights were dimmed, I had a good look at the fellow and blurted out, "You look the same as Tom, when he was about your age." He replied, "Well, Margie, thank you. That is my daddy." A new friend was made. All during intermission, he stuck right beside me and I had to tell him when and where I met his dad. He wanted a picture of us both. And there I stood with this handsome fellow, with his arm around my shoulder. I love that picture. He went backstage and told his dad about me and since Tom has a memory like an elephant, he said to his son, "You buy Margie a CD she likes." His son accompanied it with a very nice thank you note. If Tom had come out and talked to me, he would have been swamped like Elvis Presley.

A few years later, he appeared at our Heritage Festival; we always have the best entertainment. It is an outdoor concert and, of course, I was in the first row and this time I got the chance to exchange a few words with him. He made my day.

Margie Mastellar
The Red-Haired,
Dutch Counter Girl

Eddie Vedder
(The Real Guitar Hero)

Eddie Vedder is a man who has created amazing music and lyrics that have helped me through difficult times. Eddie Vedder, lead singer of Pearl Jam, has been a great American songwriter for the past 20 years. I have never met him, but I feel I have known him as a friend, for the past five years.

Eddie has taught me several lessons through his lyrical meaning and has influenced me to be a better person. His attitude towards life, and the way he presents it, is like nothing else. He has been through hard times and was able to express his feelings in his music. This has inspired me to learn guitar and try to follow in his footsteps. He is a superstar, but has stayed true to himself.

He produces music that explains the way he feels about the world and the problems with it. His opinions about the world match my opinions; his ideals match my ideals. In that way, I feel as if he is a good friend that I have known for years.

The way Eddie has touched my life, without ever knowing, makes it much more meaningful. He has greatly impacted this world in a good way. I feel that if more people thought the way he thought, this world would be a much better place for all. And that is why he is not just a hero, but a real, modern-day superhero. He can save the world, not with a weapon, but with a guitar and his voice.

James Sullivan, 16

Winston Churchill

I chose Winston Churchill, prime minister of Great Britain throughout the war years of 1939 to 1945, as my hero. We would be living in a vastly different world today, had it not been for the presence of this man.

Europe was overrun by Nazi forces at the outset of World War II. England was spared a similar fate only because of the existence of the 20-mile wide English Channel. Throughout the Battle of Britain during the years 1939 to 1945, the Blitz rained bombs on cities, dockyards, railroads, and military establishments.

Winston Churchill rallied the people of his country to stand their ground. He did this through his presence in the devastated areas of the country and his speeches defying the enemy's efforts to subdue England. This was all following the conquest of all of Europe in the opening months of World War II.

His stand and defiance was broadcast throughout the world and brought immediate support from the countries of the British Commonwealth of Nations. That support came in the form of army forces fighting in North Africa and later on the beaches of Normandy. It took the shape of naval forces defending the trade routes of the North Atlantic Ocean and air forces battling enemy formations over Britain throughout the opening years of the war and later, over continental Europe.

Considering the foregoing, I feel I speak for many when I designate Winston Churchill as my hero.

Cuthbert Gunning

Steve Omischl

Steve Omischl is my hero because he is from North Bay, Ontario, and went to my school, W.J. Fricker. He has been to the Olympics twice, and won the World Cup two years in a row. I really like his signature move of five twists and four flips (quint-twisting quad), but the most exciting thing is that he learned to ski at our tiny hill, Laurentian Ski Hill.

At Laurentian Ski Hill, I am working on rails and jumps. My favourite trick, and the hardest one, is the iron cross with grab, and then spread-eagle while doing a 360. My favourite freestyle coach is Kent Rundle because he teaches me how to do tricks. Steve also inspires me to keep trying and never give up. I met him once at the ski hill. I always watch him doing flips and spins on television. Now I freestyle ski, too, just like him and I love it very much. It is my favorite winter sport. If it wasn't for him, I wouldn't be freestyle skiing. I hope when I grow up, I can be just like him, doing spins and flips. He is awesome, even though he does not have Head skis like me.

Zach Pecore, 10

Canada's Unknown Soldier

When you're 18, the feeling is amazing. The thought of your entire life ahead of you is warming and heartening. Many Canadians have had their lives tragically cut short around this age. The worst part is that many chose to put themselves in the danger that ultimately caused their deaths. I am referring to soldiers of our nation who fought for Canada in the wars of the earth and, more specifically, World War One. My hero is Canada's Unknown Soldier.

To go off to fight in a war is, thankfully, foreign to me but even if it wasn't, I don't understand how people my age would want to go. The Unknown Soldier takes this a step farther because he died and was overlooked. Nobody knows his name, who his descendants are or where he came from. He was not a hero in the war, but simply a statistic. He is a person who sacrificed himself, without any recognition, for the peace and freedom that we, as Canadians, now take for granted.

To just lie in the fields of France for all eternity, without anyone knowing the details of your life - being insignificant - gives me the chills. Fortunately, some soldiers are given second chances. Not all of those unknown soldiers who were laid to rest in the fields of France can be brought back to Canada to be grieved upon, but one was. Because of him we remember them all and the greatest sacrifice they gave us. It's a sacrifice to this beautiful country I love, and his tomb represents all those soldiers lost.

Matt Bahm

CHAPTER ELEVEN

HEROES IN OUR SCHOOLS

*Great teachers never strive to explain
their vision. They simply invite you to
stand beside them and see for yourself.*

R. Inman

Bill Peacock (Sir)

The rooms were full again. It was another day of unend-ing tributes to a lady barely 30 years old. She lay quietly, restful it seemed, unaware of her guests and their feelings. There was time for sleep now, a luxury to her most days. It was something she never had time for.

Looking around at the mix of people, you could tell she was successful. There were people from all walks of life that loved her, her beautiful smile, her vibrant personality, and her zest for life. The list of qualities was endless. She was a true, genuine person who had made it. She found her niche in life and made a success of it.

A rebellious young girl who had risen to the challenge and beat the odds, she was proof that having one hero in your life makes the difference; one person to believe in the best of you and expect nothing less than that. A hero steps in just when almost everyone believes you're not worth it.

She was 14 and everyone was tired of her silent rage bub-bling and exploding without warning. One could never argue with the reasons as her blunt, forthright honesty gained unquestionable respect with all the authorities involved in any incident. She always owned her behaviour, but was never willing to change until Mr. Peacock and the Section 13 class at Chippewa S.S. What clicked is unknown, but looking around at all the people attending her funeral was all the proof that was needed.

Mr. Peacock, a quiet and handsome man, demanded nothing but some of the respect that he gave to each individual in his class. She called him, 'Sir', at first in mockery, but as each week went by, the label became increasingly respectful, growing more into a term of endearment.

In the months that followed, the rage subsided, allowing her softer qualities to shine through. She felt it herself. Her only fight left was to prove to the world how wrong they could be. Each step of her journey was bravely taken with fortitude and hope, not without its share of tears and hurdles that only a valiant spirit could surround. Her confidant and mentor never failed to be there in his 'Believe in Serena' campaign. They stayed in contact long after her exodus from Section 13.

Serena died of unknown medical reasons at 30 years of age. She had graduated from college with honours while raising her young daughter. She pursued her career, believing in her abilities no matter what crossed her path and it often reflected on where she had come from. She ended that career too soon, but her goal had been reached. Mr. Peacock had been right. In memory of my dear daughter, Serena, and her teacher, Mr. Peacock, her hero.

Peggy McIsaac

Marcie Gervais

My teacher, Mrs. Gervais, is a very helpful person to everyone in our class. She also helps someone in my class who has autism. She has someone to help her with him, but she helps him a lot, too.

Mrs. Gervais has a big heart and a big belly. She is having a baby soon. Her belly is really big and her belly button sticks out. It looks really funny. She is going to be a great mom because she is a great teacher and knows how to look after children.

Whenever I am stuck on my work, she always takes the time to help me and I always do well if she helps me on my work. She is great at helping all of the students to make sure everyone does well in her class.

Sometimes I hang around with her when she is doing yard duty. She is a good person to talk to. She also marks our big, long stories and all of our work from class and that is a lot of work for her.

Mrs. Gervais always has a smile on her face and she is kind to everyone.

Graeme Vaananen, 8

Carolyn Samuel
(a.k.a. Mme Sam)

Throughout your lifetime, you meet many people - people who make a difference in the world and people who have an immense amount of positivity in their character. Some will make you laugh or make you happy. Some people are fortunate enough to have another person in their life that has the power to change them. I was, and am, one of the lucky ones who was blessed to have a good person by my side. This person has a warm, kind heart and changed my life forever for the better, and it is something I will never forget. This is my story.

High school, for most, can be a difficult time. Between achieving admirable grades, planning for the future and dealing with the teenage emotions that rise and fall dramatically, it's a lot of pressure. When it comes to being understood, youth usually receive the short end of the stick.

From the age of 15 until 18, I was going through a very difficult time in my life; it was very stressful. My grades dropped considerably in school and many people noticed an emotional change in me. Many conflicting events were occurring. I drifted into a state of depression and forgot who I was. The positive, happy-go-lucky person that everyone knew in me faded away. I refrained from talking to people that used to be close to me and withdrew from the social life I once knew. I lost all my friends, my family, my hopes, my dreams, and my meaning in life. My life completely turned around for the worse.

While I was going through this rocky time, I had a remarkable person by my side, even when I didn't respond. She is a teacher who was there for me, almost like a mother. When no one else was around, Miss Carolyn Samuel, a teacher at Chippewa, was there to support me, to make me feel as if I had a purpose. She supported me, not only educationally, but emotionally as well. A miraculous person and friend, she gave me strength when I had minimal courage. The ambition I have today, I have only because of Miss Sam.

Educationally, she did much for me. I would not have picked up my grades, set goals, or become the person I am today had it not been for her. My English marks were suffering greatly.

Every day, she would say something positive to me and cheer me on to do great in school and in life. From the moment she would walk in, the classroom would be filled with positive energy. She did many things for me that teachers are not required to do. She always went the extra mile to ensure that I was happy and living up to my full potential. She not only taught me how to write outstanding opinion pieces and summaries, but she taught me something you cannot learn in school: how important it is to live from the heart and to be yourself.

Like the typical teenager, I didn't care much about my education, how I did in school, and what the future consequences would be for choosing to act this way. Miss Sam is, without a doubt, the most positive, influential person I have had the privilege to know and have in my life. She made me realize just how important an education is and how essential it is for a successful future. When I was struggling in school and in life, Miss Sam was there to guide me in the right direction.

Not only did she help me reach many goals, ultimatums, and surpass educational limits, Miss Sam inspired me to pursue a career in the art of writing. In addition to her many contributions, she helped me to achieve dreams I never thought were possible. Miss Sam has had such an empowering affect on me. To this day, I have remembered her kind, generous nature, not only with me, but with others as well. She is an amazing person who helped me through many hardships and is a phenomenal addition to humanity.

Whether it is a friend, relative, mentor, role model or teacher, big or small, short or tall - all people have the power within themselves to have an affect on another. People of all races, cultures and languages can, in some way or another, be heroic individuals. All people have great qualities in them and if everyone would use these qualities for good, and positively use them on humanity, the world would be such a beautiful, happy place for all to live in.

Kristena Carneiro-Bowman

Diane Johanson

We spent the last years of our high-school careers together. The year she retired was my last year of high school. My year went sour and I never finished. One credit shy of a high-school diploma, I failed and she retired. I haven't spoken to her since. Now in a night-school course and finally passing beyond that final stepping stone, I still crave that one lady's praise. I know that, should I see her on the street, I would receive a nudge from her fist to my chin with an, "I'm proud of you, kid."

Being approachable is one quality that not many people have; owners of that skill deserve to be commended. A guidance counsellor listens to what you have to say, gives advice on your career path and once in a while, follows up on career goals. They then set new goals and keep records. I had never approached adults for this type of help until I met the right helper, Diane Johanson. She was the counsellor at Widdifield Secondary who represented a shoulder to cry on, an ear to listen, and a heart full of great advice.

High school is a place where every child is expected to have a sense of where they are going in life. Without it, you have a different one: the sense of being lost. I never had the problem of lacking a goal; I had the problem of having too many. Through all of the changes that I never anticipated, Mrs. Johanson re-directed me. I was never able to hold onto one dream. She realistically supported me through each and every change.

Looking back, I remember three separate occasions that brought me into her office. The first was about another girl in my class. I could tell there was something wrong with her little body and I approached her because I wanted to help. After a lengthy discussion, I could not turn away. This led me into the office where I explained the young girl's situation and demanded something be done. Mrs. Johanson's reply was that she was already doing the best she could. I should have known that, where Mrs. Johanson could help, she already had. The second memory of her office pertained to a career choice. I expected to hear words of mild discouragement. Instead, after telling her I wanted to become a family physician, she laid out the strategy I needed in order to succeed. Someone who hardly knew me believed in me. This is when I developed the true respect I never had for a teacher. Without these two occasions, I would not have had the third. I remember bringing a letter to her office, shortly before her retirement. This letter thanked her for her help, her friendship, and her unfathomable guidance and wished her a wonderful retirement. Something tells me she still has that piece of paper, tucked away.

Finally, when our paths resembled the dividing line of that second-last letter of the alphabet, I had no inspiration. I slowly untangled and lost all the dreams that I had worked for. Two years later, I have re-energized and am working towards the diploma I need and will move on to be a high-school teacher. Hopefully, I will be one that has at least half of the enthusiasm, encouragement, and heart that she does. She never gave up and because of that, she fights in me every day. Thank you, Mrs. Johanson, for giving me the example I needed.

Chelsey Brown

Dawn Antonissen

My grade-nine geography teacher, Ms. Antonissen, has done a lot to help me through the past few months. I have had a few ups and downs and she has done everything she can to get me back on my feet.

Right now, I am in foster care and have been in this position for almost a year. I have had so many days when I felt that I was worthless and just wanted to give up on everything. However, Ms. Antonissen has made that difference for me. She has shown me that life gets harder and harder, but she believes I can make it better by staying strong. No matter what happens day-to-day, I just have to remember that a lot of people love me for who I am, even though I have made mistakes.

A lot of people have thrown me away but, like Ms. Antonissen says, people make mistakes and learn from them. It is true that people learn from their mistakes. I just wish that the people closest to me who have thrown me away would realize and understand what I have done to help myself. I want them to know I cannot change my past but I can change my future.

Getting thrown into life like this is the hardest thing, but when you have an amazing and wonderful person like Ms. Antonissen in your life and she is there for you each and every day with a great big smile on her face, you know you can beat anything. I thank you for that.

Rebecca-Ann Gagné, 16

Mike Wright
(Meant to Be)

To some students, a teacher is no more than another face in the crowd and one that they feel is rather unimportant. He is simply the person who stands at the front of the classroom each day and talks about a variety of things, none of which the students are interested in. I'm not one of those students. As a matter of fact, I'm exactly the opposite. My teachers are some of the most important people in my life, but this story is about one specific high-school teacher, named Mike Wright.

I first met Mike when I decided to take part in the Athletic Council at my high school in grade 10. Mike was the staff advisor for the council and even though I didn't know anyone else who was participating, he welcomed me as if we had known each other for years. Our personalities matched right off the bat and we developed more than just a student-teacher relationship; we became real friends.

In grade 11, I became vice-president of the Athletic Council and was also enrolled in a physical geography class with Mike. We spent many hours before and after school, as well as on the weekends, preparing for different sporting events in the school and running the canteen at other school events. In class, Mike was always a very animated teacher who strongly encouraged student participation and made every lesson stand out in its own way. Since I really enjoyed his class in grade 11, I chose to take another class with him in grade 12. He was just as enthusiastic. I was elected president of the Athletic Council that year and spent even more hours working with Mike at all the events throughout the year.

Over those three years in high school, Mike was my role model, my hero. I spent more time volunteering and working with him than I did with some of my own friends! I'm now studying at Nipissing University and plan to become a teacher or perhaps a professor. I credit Mike with helping me make the best decision of my entire life: the decision to move to North Bay and study geography at Nipissing. Mike graduated from Nipissing with degrees in both geography and education. I feel as though I'm following in his footsteps. I'm in the same program and I have taken an interest in many of the same clubs and activities as he did when he was here. Mike is a fantastic teacher and he has inspired me to want to do the same. He is always involved at the school, not only in teaching, but in many extracurricular activities. This is the type of teacher I wish to become and he inspires me to succeed here at Nipissing so that I can be just like him. It is a decision that I'm proud of every single day and I hope that he is proud of me, as well.

This coming year will be my third year at Nipissing and I still regularly keep in touch with Mike. He has helped me discover many things about Nipissing that I might not have found out on my own and has helped me make many important contacts within the university. We still organize events together through the university as I'm a member of the student-alumni club on campus and each event brings back memories of the old times in high school. When I go back home, I always make sure I visit Mike at the high school since he is an important person in my life. Perhaps one day, we will be co-workers at my old high school or alumni board members together at Nipissing. Either way, Mike is a great friend, a great teacher and a great role model.

Jodie King

Gina Armstrong-Aro

The woman who has most inspired my life is Ms. Gina Armstrong-Aro. She has been one of my dance teachers since I started at Widdifield Secondary School four years ago. She made a profound statement to me the other day: "I am a victor... not a victim. I am not a survivor because I have conquered cancer." She approaches life with this positive outlook. This bout with cancer was an inspiration and a motivation to her, to live life to the fullest. She was diagnosed with cancer 10 years ago. When she received the news of her illness, her first thought was, "the show must go on." She was not going to let the illness beat her.

Mrs. A. continued to work and started planning her treatment. When the radiation therapy began, she had to take a leave of absence from work. She had to go to Toronto to see specialists and live with other people. The doctors performed a skin graft, taking skin from her abdomen and placing it on her foot. She had to go through rehabilitation and recuperation for almost a full year, to be healthy again. She told me that her dog was the best therapy she ever had. Doctors told her that she would never dance again, but she refused to believe that and kept working on her strength and flexibility. She beat the odds and she is still dancing to this day!

Ms. Armstrong-Aro has influenced me by showing me courage. In my opinion, it took a lot of courage to go back to teaching a dance class just after finding out that you have been diagnosed with cancer. I can only imagine the strength and determination it took for her to battle this disease and conquer it.

Another way that she has influenced me is that, throughout her turmoil, she always retained her composure. The best way to describe her is "regal". When I see how she conducts herself, I try to model myself after her. I always try to conduct myself like a lady and in a manner that would make her proud.

Her illness and her life experiences have also taught me the value of determination and having a positive attitude. I have seen the scar that cancer surgery left behind, but you can hardly notice it because she has such personal presence. Her story impresses me so much because she has made me realize that I can achieve any goal that I set for myself. She makes me believe that no dream is impossible, as long as you work hard to achieve it.

Her life story and my interaction with her have taught me respect for others and most of all, for myself. She treats all her students fairly and equally and I try to emulate her in my daily activities. Her experience with cancer also taught her humility and this trait is something that she stresses to all her students. We are not superior or inferior to the next person. We are all beautiful and all equal to each other.

Finally, this amazing teacher has influenced my life by teaching me the value of family and friends. During her illness, her family and friends supported her and gave her strength to be victorious over her illness. Her experience has taught me that family and friends are the backbone that we rely on to get us through our lives.

Cheyanne Helson

Erin Robertson

Can you imagine being pregnant, being stuck in an uncomfortably hot room, and teaching a class who just won't listen, but still being a great teacher to those who do? The reason I can is because I have a teacher like that. Every day is the same thing: the kids that are late argue that they're not and when class starts, they just keep talking. You get the message? Her name is Mrs. Robertson. She has put up with that every day! I don't know how she does it.

I'm always the one at the back of the class saying, "Guys, have some respect." But lately, this hasn't been working well. One day, I had just reached my limit and was extremely close to tears. Mrs. Robertson talked to me after class and told me it wasn't my fault; I still felt horrible. The kids went from ignoring me to calling me, and sometimes my friends, horrible names. My days were always ruined until that day when Mrs. Robertson took me aside. She reassured me that I wasn't to blame and that I wasn't those things that the kids had called me, and that she wasn't hurt by the kids because what they wanted was to get her angry.

I left class that day feeling better and knowing that my favorite teacher wasn't getting abused. She was only getting stronger. For this, I respect her and admire her for everything she stands for. I just hope that one day, the kids that love to torment Mrs. Robertson mature a bit and give some respect. Mrs. Robertson, you're my hero.

Amanda Mitchell, 15

Editor's Note: Erin, her husband Mark, and her daughter Neve, welcomed baby Molly Robertson into the world on Monday, August 13th, 2007. Congrats!

Colette Landry
(A Dedicated Educational Assistant)

It took a lot of patience, frustration, many tests, and minor surgery before I was blessed with my beautiful daughter. Megan was born with blue eyes, blond hair, and a really round face. The gynecologist called her "the miracle baby". She was to be my only child.

Megan was a very good baby. She slept well, ate well, and smiled a lot. At about age one-and-a-half, she was going non-stop, from early morning to late evening. She was hyperactive and had no sense of danger. Daycare workers, who were used to children, as well as doctors, confirmed my worries: she had special needs.

Over the years, she has had many different diagnoses: ADHD, verbal dyspraxia, autism, not autism, and now, pervasive development disorder, non-otherwise specified (PDD-NOS). She's had to be accompanied in the school setting by a full-time educational assistant, being supervised at all times. She's had much difficulty concentrating and behaving appropriately in a classroom of peers. She has been, at times, quite disruptive and disturbing to other children, sometimes having to be removed to a quiet place to be redirected to task or simply re-focus.

A few short years ago at St-Anne's school in North Bay, Megan, being her normal hyperactive self, was having lunch under the supervision of her educational assistant, Colette Landry. Colette had persevered with Megan for three years.

Without knowing Megan, it is hard to imagine the quantity of patience it required and the many frustrations encountered along the way. I always tried to provide Megan with a nutritious lunch and healthy snacks, avoiding sugar as best I could. That one fateful day, she was eating grapes and perhaps not paying very much attention to chewing before swallowing. One grape lodged itself in her throat, instantly blocking her airway. Her eyes grew big and her hands went instinctively to her throat. Colette, having had proper training, quickly went around Megan and performed the Heimlich maneuver. The grape, along with some of her lunch, was evacuated onto the floor. Megan began hyperventilating, trying to get her breath back. She had had a big scare. Colette managed to calm her, while her own insides were pretty shaken. She dutifully reported to the principal the incident that had just occurred. Megan had had a close call but luckily, had been in the care of someone with the appropriate training. I could not help but wonder what if, that day, it had not been Colette with her, but a person that had not had the training necessary for this particular emergency? That could easily happen to any child, at any time, at any school.

Following the incident, I asked the principal if we could have a presentation at the school. She quickly approved. I then contacted our M.P., at the time Bob Wood, and also The North Bay Nugget. I wanted to explain to all the children how quickly something like that could happen and the importance of knowing what to do to save someone from choking. I had Megan explain in her own words what had happened to her. We had all the students' undivided attention. Bob Wood presented Colette with certificates of appreciation from the Nipissing Riding and also from Prime Minister Jean Chrétien. It was all to honour Colette, before the students and her co-workers, for that moment that made a difference in Megan's life, as well as mine.

Megan is now functioning in a special needs classroom with a few other children and another very dedicated educational assistant. She is learning behaviour and social skills, along with life skills that she will need to have to function in today's society as an adult. She still does not, to this day, eat any grapes.

Nicole Bucknell

Some Special Students
(A Teacher's Blessings)

The call was heard across North Bay for stories about local heroes - people who change lives. As I sat down to rock my five-month-old boy, Nate, to sleep, I, too, drifted off thinking of mine. It took only a moment for 11 beautiful children's faces to smile back at me.

As a special education teacher in the Learning Assistance Centre at John XXIII Catholic School, I have the privilege of being a daily part of my students' lives. These children all have multiple exceptionalities (autism, physical and intellectual disabilities, cerebral palsy, blindness) which have never dimmed their fighting spirits.

Each day, these children fight their way through simple tasks which we, many times, take for granted. In their non-assuming way, they demonstrate that life is filled with small joys that need to be cherished, as well as celebrated, each day. When life brings forth obstacles and challenges that I wish not to face alone, I simply need to look at these small heroes and I am reminded of their positive energy and their determination to face what life has given them. These moments provide me with the strength I need to continue on.

When thinking about heroes, one often thinks of people who, through their heroic acts or kind gestures, change other people's lives. My students do not have the ability to speak or run to save another from harm. It is through living life joyfully each day, despite their disabilities, that they demonstrate their true heroism.

They face adversity and challenges each moment of their lives. My students inspire all those around them to smile through life's challenges and to be thankful for all that we have been blessed with. Since starting as a special education teacher, I have continuously been inspired by my students to be the best that I can be and to be the true hero in my own life. My calling as a teacher has proven to be a blessing. Not only do I get to teach children with a variety of exceptionalities, but each day I am reminded of the true spirit of life.

Cindy Luesby-Gravelle

CHAPTER TWELVE

OUR FAMILIES

What greater thing is there for human souls than to feel that they are joined for life - to be with each other in silent unspeakable memories.

George Eliot

Greg and Gail Samuel
(Of Yahtzee and Things)

I've learned to dodge the looks of confusion and the sarcastic comments of disapproval. The nay-Sayers can't shake me. Those who don't get it need not trouble themselves with the creative put downs. I, like my parents, am faithful and committed. We gather on a weekly basis (more often on holidays) and ritually situate ourselves around the kitchen table. We each have an assigned chair, a favourite pen, and a strategy for winning that we separately feel is flawless. Of course, the standard Milton Bradley-issued score sheet that seems to satisfy millions of happy participants simply would not do for our household. We more serious players had to custom design a ten-game score sheet aptly named, "The Samuel Yahtzee Board". We added on some bonus large straights and changed some of the values. And no, we don't play one game at a time, but all ten at once. So, when we settle into our assigned Yahtzee posts, clutching our writing utensils and manipulating the dice between our fingers, we mean business. Now why, you ask, would a 30-year-old woman get such genuine joy out of playing a game designed for children of six? That's quite simple. It's the company.

When I look around the table, I see two people that I love so much I could cry. Maybe it's because I was loved so much in the first place. I still remember the confusion I felt when I learned that the sun does not physically rise and set according to my bedtime.

My father, Greg, did the standard dad stuff for me and my brothers, Kevin and Mark. He taught us how to swim and fish. He made my stuffed animals dance and gave them funny voices. He read me bedtime stories and told me in a deep voice of absolute certainty that I could be anything I wanted. That's why it came as an incredible shock to me when I learned of the horrible things he endured as a child. I had no idea. I remember I was in my late teens when he first told me stories of abuse that were a sharp and brutal contrast to my own upbringing. He sheltered me from it. How does a man who was raised with little money, little food, little love, little education, and no parents from the age of 15, learn to break the abusive cycle? He truly is a remarkable human being, full of endearing qualities. It is because of him that I understand the resiliency of the human spirit.

And then I look to his right and see my mother, Gail. She knows more than anyone I know about how to keep a loving household running smoothly. She budgets, she cleans, she runs errands, she cooks and, most impressive, she raised me and my brothers up from runny-nosed, bare-footed rug rats into well-rounded adults. And with all she does, to this day, she can barely accept a compliment or buy something new for herself, despite my best efforts. Yet, she has no problem staying up with us when we're sick or coming to the rescue when we're burning a roast.

The standard Yahtzee game is 90 minutes and, in our opinion, not all is based on the luck of the rolls, but rather the strategic placing of the scores on the grid. The game would take longer, I'm sure, if played by 'amateurs' who waste time adding the five dice, but we're trained to know at a glance the total of the cubes as they fall. As I sit here and think about how lucky I am, how loved I am, and how I will always be welcome at this table, I know I can't possibly express all that my parents, Greg and Gail Samuel, actually mean to me. So I think I'll stop now and get back to our game.

Carolyn Samuel

Hayley Sebalj

When choosing a hero, many people select someone that they know personally. Mine is a little different. She is my older sister, Hayley, who I've never met.

When Hayley was born on May 15, 1991, everyone was so excited for my parents. It was their first child! Shortly after, excitement turned to tear-filled eyes and hearts full of sympathy when the doctor said the four words that every parent dreads hearing, "she didn't make it".

Just a few months ago, my cousin had to hear those exact four words. I stood outside, a week later, and waited for the funeral to be over. I watched my own family walk outside and cry. My mom walked back to the car. Everyone told her that she shouldn't go, but she went because she felt she had to be there for my cousin.

On that day, I realized what an impact Hayley had made on my parents and on me. I got home that night and looked through Hayley's photo album. There was not a smile on a face. There was nothing but confusion. At the back of the album, there was her handprint. I put my hand over it and, for that second, I found my sister. She was somewhere I never would've looked. She's in me.

Hayley's death showed me how I need to be there for my younger brother. Hayley's death has also shown me what a good role model my mom has been. The doctors told my mom she would never get pregnant. Not long after that, she gave birth to Hayley. A year later, she was pregnant again and in November, 1992, she gave birth to me. Another four and a half years later in March of 1997, she gave birth to my younger brother, Jake. My mom almost died giving birth to Jake. But by the smile she wears every day, you would never know that she went through all of that.

Growing up, my mom was told she wouldn't be a good mother, but I know I couldn't have asked for better. If it wasn't for Hayley's passing, I don't think I would have ever realized any of this. No one talks about Hayley, but I feel that her spirit lives on and she's watching over me because she waited for me to find her. It took 14 years, but not once did she give up on me.

Kayla Sebalj, 14

Sarah Welton
(You Had Me at Hello!)

Several years back, when my children were quite small, I was a very busy mother. I preached kindness to others, the importance of manners, how every one of us has some-thing to offer. I imagined myself a decent person - caring, well-mannered, accepting of others, non-judgmental. Yes, a good role model, setting a good example for my children.

It was an otherwise normal visit to the Neurology Clinic in Toronto at the Hospital for Sick Children. In North Bay, it is easy to feel unique with your situation when there are few families to compare with. However, at this hospital, you are humbled as you observe the many children and their families that crowd the building. My husband and I had our family in tow, a child held with each hand, stepping along with the giant yellow footprints towards the Neurology Wing, right on-schedule for their medical check-ups. We corralled our gang into the waiting room, placing ourselves near the toys and television. I mentally rehearsed, recalling the suggestions mentioned last visit; did we have any successes to report? It is stressful, but important, to be prepared with any questions or concerns. I remembered to bring my calendar/journal to refer to. Other families joined us in the waiting area. Intense faces of the parents mirrored back at us. Do they feel prepared? I couldn't help but notice them, making a quick mental assess-ment of what their possible situation might be. It is a momen-tary distraction from my mental prep before our name is called.

We had to be waiting, maybe, 15 minutes. I looked up when a middle-aged woman approached, pushing a girl in a wheelchair. I gasped at the girl's appearance! Oh, my God, what happened to her? Is she in the right clinic? The woman parked the girl directly in front of my oldest daughter, Sarah, and me and then went to sign in at the clinic desk. I awkwardly tried to look, without being obvious. I curiously observed her to be around 15 years old, maybe more; it was hard to tell. She sat in the wheelchair, leaning to the right, with her head looking down at her lap. On her lap, she was holding a backpack, covered with stickers. She wore glasses that tilted to the right side, the same direction that her head tilted. Looking at her head, I detected a huge, bald section at the right front, where hair normally would have covered. Several scars were visible edging this bald section. What hair she did have was thin, stringy, and brown. Her right forehead, directly above her eye, appeared collapsed. I thought, possibly, she'd had part of her brain removed. It distorted the shape around her right eye. I wondered if she had full vision in that eye. I imagined how hard it might be for her family. What have they been through? What was everyday life like for them? I imagined that the girl must require a lot of care. It frightened me to think...

Instantly and without hesitation, Sarah jumped out of her seat and walked right up to the side of the wheelchair. I was so self-absorbed that I hadn't noticed Sarah's interest. I held my breath, fearing an embarrassing moment coming on. What disfigured body part was she going to ask about? - What happened to your hair? Or, what's wrong with you? To my astonishment and absolute delight, my daughter gleefully spoke, "Hi, I'm Sarah! What's your name?" The girl spontaneously lifted her head and, with a huge, ear-to-ear smile, said, "I'm Sandra!" There wasn't even a pause as Sarah continued, "Wow, you sure have a lot of stickers. Can you show me? Where did you get them all?"

It took only seconds for these two children to connect, not about medical conditions, struggles, or limitations in life, but about those fabulous stickers! I tried to smile, but teared up with emotion instead. I was so proud of my daughter. Sarah was so sincere and wonderful. Her approach was so dignified, so respectful, so natural. What a lesson for me. She totally looked past the features that I saw as barriers. That moment forever changed the way that I approach people. I knew my daughter had set the example on how to see the person first, not the disability. Thank you, Sarah.

Jo-Anne Welton

Chris Cowan

My hero is my big brother, Chris. He is 15 years old and the best role model and brother a girl could ever want. He is five years older than me. I have a story to tell about how he became my hero.

I was six years old and he was 11. It was a hot, summer night and my window was open. Earlier, I had brought a glass of water to bed with me and went to sleep. Then, at 2 a.m., I woke up and reached for my water to find a DEAD BEE in it! I, being extremely scared of bees, was terrified. So, I ran into Chris' room at 2 a.m. and woke him up by repeatedly saying, "Chris, there's a bee in my drink. Help me, help me, help me!" And Chris, seeing my scaredness, well, helped me. He went into my room, picked up my water, went into the bathroom, and flushed the bee down the toilet! "Bye-bye bee." I said, relieved.

Ever since then, my big brother, Chris, was my hero and still is for that reason and more. I worried when he broke his collar bone. I worried when the doctor said it had to be fixed with surgery and I cried when I saw him after the surgery. I love my brother.

Samantha Cowan, 10

Jennifer Richmond

In April 2006, my 16-year-old daughter, Jennifer, was diagnosed with Ewing Sarcoma, a form of cancer. For a year, she had had a lot of pain in her right arm. After a CAT scan was ordered, we were told she had a shanoma tumour and that it wasn't cancer. By the time Jenny was operated on in Ottawa, the tumour had pressed on her nerve supply and she was paralyzed on the right side of her body.

After the surgery, her dad, my oldest daughter, Mandy, and I were taken into a room by the doctor and told that Jenny did indeed have cancer. I will never forget Jenny's reaction when we told her. There were a few tears and then she looked at us and said, "That's okay, I'll beat it." They moved her to the CHEO Hospital for children and there we started a year that I will never forget. The shock of finding out that your daughter has cancer is bad enough, but then they told us that because the cancer was so aggressive, they would have to start the chemo and radiation immediately. Jenny had a month of radiation and a year of chemo. She was very sick during her treatments and she went down to 83 pounds at one point.

I remember sitting by her bed when they had to put an NG tube in her nose to try to feed her and thinking, 'what I wouldn't do to change places with her'. When she was vomiting from the chemo, I would stand outside her room sometimes and cry and cry. One time, I went back into her room and she said, "What's wrong, mommy?" I told her that I wished with all my heart that I could change places with her and take all the pain away. She laughed and said she didn't because I was old and I wouldn't be able to fight the cancer. All my daughter should have had to worry about this year was making sure she graduated, picking out her prom dress, and talking her dad into renting her a limo. Instead, she had chemo and radiation that made her so sick, she lost all of her hair, and she will never get the use of her right arm back, ever.

Jenny had a dream of becoming a nurse, a dream that will never come true now. When Jenny was diagnosed, I lost my job and my apartment, but we were both blessed to have been able to live at Ronald McDonald House, next to CHEO Hospital in Ottawa. Jenny was in the hospital for six months straight; the love and support of the staff at Ronald McDonald House, and the other families that I met that were going through the same thing, got me through this. Jenny's doctors and nurses at CHEO were also amazing, as was one lady in particular, the inter-link nurse, Marilyn Cassidy. She went beyond the call of duty and her caring and loving support is there for every oncology family that walks through the doors of that hospital.

During Jenny's time in CHEO, she made some wonderful friends. There was one in particular, Eric Shaw. They became very close and then, in January this year, Eric passed away. Jenny and I saw so many children lose the battle, but she never gave up or let her positive way of thinking diminish. Jenny was an amazing support to many of the younger children in the hospital. She would explain to them what it was like to lose their hair and many of them, after talking to Jenny, weren't afraid anymore. She had also made a video with Eric and his schoolmates, for a telethon they were having at their school. At Eric's celebration of life, she got up in front of many people and told them what Eric meant to her and I was so very proud of her. Jenny also befriended a little seven-year-old girl, Hannah, who also lived at Ronald McDonald House with us for the past year. She did everything with Hannah. Whether it was watching Hannah's favourite show, 'Hannah Montana', or reading or watching a movie or doing arts and crafts, they were always together. Hannah and her family and Jenny and I have become very, very close. You see, the friends - no - the family you make at Ronald McDonald House is a family forever! It is truly 'The House that Love Built'. Jenny was also asked to co-host the CHEO Telethon with Max Keeping, and she did an interview for the Nugget for the Relay for Life, as well as an interview with COGECO.

Jenny will also be doing the opening ceremonies speech at the Relay for Life this year and, as she said today, she is just going to 'wing it'. My daughter is an amazing young lady. She turned 18 on May 21st and because of a lot of hard work during her treatments, she will be graduating with all of her friends from St. Joseph's Scollard-Hall on June 18th. I don't know how she made it through this horrible nightmare. At times, I didn't think I could make it without her. Jenny, you are an inspiration to us all! Keep up that positive attitude. You are an amazing person, friend, sister, niece, granddaughter, and most importantly, daughter. I love you with all my heart, Jenny!

Love, always and forever, Mom

Ann Richmond

Jeremy Harkness

I know that if Jeremy were still here, he would be so excited to see that his picture is on the cover of a book with his "girlfriend", Jenny Richmond, of the previous story. He was an amazing child. You could read a whole world of stories just by looking into Jeremy's big, beautiful, blue eyes.

Jeremy was diagnosed with Neuroblastoma on his third birthday. Doctors found a large tumour that weighed a pound and a half in his left abdomen. Between July 2006 and January 2007, Jeremy's scans were coming out clean. The next scan of the new year told a different story. A tumour had grown and hidden itself between his kidney and his spine.

Jeremy went through six cycles of intense chemo, getting subsequently weaker and sicker with each cycle. In August of this year, Jeremy went to Toronto Sick-Kids for a stem cell implant. His immune system depleted completely. The last day of his chemo, Jeremy tested positive for a virus that, to us, would be like the common cold. The antibiotics to treat the virus shut Jeremy's kidneys down. He was later admitted to the Critical Care Unit where he ran on dialysis 24-hours straight. The morning of September 7th, the doctor called me to tell me that Jeremy's right pupil had dilated. He had started bleeding in his brain and slipped into a coma early that morning.

In an attempt to relieve pressure on his brain, Jeremy underwent two long brain surgeries. At 2 p.m. the next day, Jeremy's neurosurgeon came in and informed us that Jeremy was brain dead and that there was nothing else they could do. After hearing this, I just wanted to grab him out of that hospital bed and bring him home, where he didn't have a care in the world. An hour later, the doctor brought my family into a small room, sat us down and started by saying "There's no easy way to say this," then added, "I'm very sorry to tell you that Jeremy is dead."

Hearing those words were like getting stabbed in the chest. There was nothing that could be done. Jeremy was at peace and without any more pain or suffering. He had successfully undergone his stem cell implant and was in remission when he passed away. Jeremy won his battle against cancer. He, just like Jenny Richmond, is a true hero and he fought everyday to make it through. He is our angel and I know that he is watching over us every day.

Krista Harkness

Jeremy's mom

Jeremy was indeed Jenny's little boyfriend and she could always make him smile. They had an amazing connection and I believe that even now they still have that connection. He is watching over Jenny and I believe he is her Guardian Angel! We loved him so very, very much and there won't be a day that will go by that we won't think about him or miss him deeply.

Ann Richmond

Jennifer's mom

Michael Bubnich

Having known Michael Bubnich for over 30 years, I have come to appreciate him and have tried to emulate so many of his fine qualities. My father-in-law is a kind, generous, honest, and hard-working man who loves his family unconditionally. Whatever the task or occasion, he is always there with a genuine smile and generous heart. Over the years, I have secretly regarded him as my guardian angel because he is always there when I need him.

I have known Michael for more than half of my life and I cannot begin to list all of his thoughtful, unselfish, and considerate actions. He is also a very humble individual who probably would be embarrassed if he knew I was singing his praises. He is my friend, he is my mentor, and he is truly a hero . . . my hero.

Des Anthony

Nicholas Fung

When my brother was born, I was almost four years old. I remember running to meet my mom in the hospital and her waiting for me in the elevator in her pajamas. I can remember pretending to feed my dolls when my mom gave my brother his milk and not understanding why he couldn't play with me, yet. As he got older, he became much like the average toddler: crazy and energetic, with way too much energy for our family and a tendency to run into any object that might be in his way. He would often drive us crazy by banging on pots and pans and he would constantly have to be watched to ensure that he didn't get into any trouble.

When he was about four and just starting school, it became clear that something was wrong. He could barely talk, though most children his age were already talking quite clearly. He had trouble grasping even the simplest ideas and was nowhere close to being able to tie his own shoes, though most of his peers were well on their way to being able to do many tasks themselves.

My parents took my brother to a doctor to find out why he was so delayed. That was when we first found out that my brother had what the doctors called a learning disability. I can remember my mom coming into my room, lying on my bed, and explaining to me that Nicholas was a little different and that they would have to have more special time with him than with my sister and me and that he required so much more attention. I was only eight, and could barely understand how these things would affect my life and my brother's life.

As he got older, Nicholas' disability slowly progressed and became more noticeable. At first, he was diagnosed with ADHD, but he was later diagnosed with a panic and anxiety disorder, as well as mild autism. He started out in a regular class, although he did have an educational assistant throughout his years at Vincent Massey. By the time he was nine, my parents decided to move him to a special class at Marshall Park so he could be surrounded by people just like him and get the help he needed. The class he is currently in does not cover subjects like geography, social studies, or sciences. His class covers solely the things he needs to know to be able to live on his own. He has learned to read, write, and do simple math.

This jump to the special class, however much it has helped, had life-changing results. He is no longer able to go back into the mainstream schools. He will be in classes like the one he is in now for the rest of his life. He will probably never graduate high school and never be able to attend college or university. He will most likely never move beyond a grade-six level of intelligence and will probably always be dependent on other people.

Unfortunately, being in the "special" class cannot protect him from the sad truths of the world we live in or from the cruelty of other children. I can still remember when he came home, one day, and announced to us that some kid had tried to beat him up, or another day when he told us that some kids had shoved him into a puddle, or pushed him into a snow bank.

Despite all this, many people do not even notice that my brother is, perhaps, a little 'different', though they do think he is much younger then he really is. I am so incredibly proud of Nicholas for being able to overcome all of his differences so that he can live a fairly normal life. He is so happy and is lots of fun to be around. At times, you can't even tell that he might be different from everyone else. He has made friends and is learning to read and write - a huge accomplishment. He works so hard to acquire the skills that come so easily to most of us, things we don't even realize we're doing, such as making eye contact when talking to people, or thinking before he speaks so that he doesn't say something he might regret.

Though he can be quite a nuisance at times, I love my brother so much. It is often hard to remember that he does not see things the same as I do and that he doesn't understand as much as we do. Yet living with him is perhaps my most valuable learning experience. It is so interesting to see his point of view on things as he notices the tiniest things, such as the buzzing of a fan or a particularly interesting design; things that most of us wouldn't take heed of. I remember being at a university and he noticed a sculpture of a man that was placed horizontally on the ceiling, which was something that I would never have noticed by myself. I cannot imagine life without my brother, without all his little quirks and the differences that make him unique.

Rachel Fung, 14

My Dog Sheena

My dog, Sheena, always made me smile. She was my best friend in the whole world.

One day I came home crying because my friends were being mean and picking on me. I opened the door and put my bags down and went downstairs. I stood in the doorway, looking at my dog, telling her I wish I had friends who were not mean and who didn't fight. Sheena barked and ran up to me. When I bent down, she put her paws up on my neck and put her head on my shoulder. It gave me the biggest smile that day. It was like Sheena gave me a hug and understood what I said.

When I wanted to go downtown or somewhere, I had to bring my dog with me just in case someone tried to hurt me or steal me. If someone tried to do something to me, I know my dog would save me.

Sheena was a dog who was spoiled. She got lots of attention and we melted cheese on her dog food (don't worry, she never got sick). She also got BIG ice cubes in her water dish. Even though Sheena is not with us anymore, whenever I am sad, I just think about her and smile.

Madison Waller, 11

Mark Gilligan
(Everyday Hero)

By the time I met Mark, I was pretty much broken. There was a profound emptiness in my heart and, in fact, my house. I'd been living in an empty house since separating from my husband. It was a simple agreement: he got all the furniture; I got the house, complete with all the debt. The kids had long-since grown and moved on with their own lives. I felt like I was an excess person on the earth; without purpose or plan, simply existing from day to day.

I had a dresser, a piano, and a treadmill that had been left behind. I scraped together enough money to purchase a bed on the day he moved out. I ate my meals standing up at the kitchen counter. I had no pots - he had taken all the pots. My salary barely covered the mortgage, heat, hydro, and car payments, but I was determined to stay in the house that I loved.

After the separation from a turbulent marriage, I never realized that a person could cry as much as I cried during those first few months. I cried myself to sleep. I awoke with tears in my eyes. I cried when they played love songs on the radio. I cried at work, sometimes. I cried in the shower. I cried all the time.

Still, I was managing to finish the curling season and the people there were kind and gentle to me. And it was in this atmosphere, at a late-winter bonspiel, that I first spoke with Mark. I ended up sitting beside him, watching one of the games. He was soft-spoken. We chatted and the conversation eventually turned to me. I found myself telling him about my situation, leaving out the worst of the details. He watched me with his deep-blue eyes and I could see concern and compassion in their depths. His face was chiseled and handsome and he looked like a man who liked to spend a lot of time outdoors. I wasn't looking for a date, but it was nice to sit and chat.

One of the biggest challenges of being alone in the country was getting the water to my horses in the winter. As a petite lady, carrying two two-and-a-half-foot-high buckets out to the horses, morning and night, was difficult at best and somewhat dangerous. And this year, with the extreme cold compounded by record snowfalls, I was spending most of my energy trying to stay ahead of the snow that constantly fell from the barn roof in front of the door!

It was a few days later when another two feet of snow had fallen, that I drove home, dreading the work at hand. Just getting up my driveway was usually a chore, but I turned in and the driveway had already been ploughed! I got out of the car and went into the house to change into my barn clothes and headed out with the buckets sloshing at my side, yet again. I set the buckets down and looked around in amazement. The pathway to the door had been neatly shoveled. It looked like a small road! I then turned to climb the embankment to the water trough. Here, there was a series of steps chiseled into the snow and ice, instead of the usual treacherous ice bank; six perfectly-formed snow steps to the water trough. Oh, such beautiful steps! I found myself smiling and I carried the buckets up the steps to empty them into the trough. I no longer felt like a middle-aged lady in an old, ragged, barn coat, with buckets but instead like a snow queen surrounded by an ice castle. Then I noticed that on the door there was a note, 'Surprise!' it said. It was signed, 'Mark'. As the months passed, Mark and I became true friends and he saw me through the most difficult times of my life. He fed me and clothed me. He held me when I cried and helped me to see the goodness in the world again. And yet, he also kept his distance, allowing me the personal space and dignity required for emotional healing to occur.

A few years later, we decided to marry and today, as my husband, he holds me with tenderness whenever the ghosts of the past haunt me. I look around my house, which now overflows with love, and have a hard time remembering those empty, empty months. I even have pots and furniture again. Mark didn't rescue me from a burning building or save me from falling off a cliff, but there isn't any doubt in my mind that he saved me from near-death just the same. And each day when I watch him carry the buckets of water out to the horses in the winter, I remember the day when I discovered those wonderful steps in the snow, sculpted with tenderness by my everyday hero.

Sally Kidson

Heather Ballentine

For as long as I can remember, I have always looked up to my sister, Heather, not just because she is my sister but because she is my role model and someone I can talk to about anything. As we grew up, we grew further apart from each other, but I knew that, no matter what, I would be able to talk to her and ask her for help whenever I needed it.

I remember going into her room late at night, after my mom had put me to bed, and we would talk for hours and hours about her life and mine, even though my life didn't have much meaning at that time. Everything that we talked about on those nights has helped me with my life now, by my not taking the wrong roads that I might have taken otherwise. I have always been able to use what she has given me to help my life, or someone else's life, and learn from it.

I use what I have learned to show her that she has a huge impact on my life and I am never going to forget that. As we live our lives now, we don't have that much time to talk to each other and just be sisters, but I want to show her what a great sister I can be to her.

Holly Elizabeth Ballentine

CHAPTER THIRTEEN

OUR GRADES THREE AND FOUR

I'm not rushing to be in love. I'm finding fourth grade hard enough.

Regina - Age 10

Sherry Semeniuk
(There for Me Every Step)

Aunt Sherry was there for me when I was born and has been there for me ever since. When I was born, Daddy wasn't comfortable standing beside the doctor to watch me come out, so Aunt Sherry took his place and was the first person in my family to see me. Since then, she has cared for me each summer for a special week-long visit in Ottawa. I always know I can count on her when I need someone to talk to. She never forgets my birthday and visits me on special occasions.

Something that I really like about Aunt Sherry is that she makes things fun by acting like a kid. She puts a special effort into making everything we do together adventurous, like painting our faces for my first Ottawa Senators game and cheering like a true Senators hockey fan with me.

She is always happy and takes the time to find out what makes me happy. We have a lot of fun together, being silly and never worrying about what others think about what we are doing. She is my godmother, but also one of my best friends.

In addition to having fun together, Aunt Sherry also teaches me many things. She often takes me to educational and fun places like museums, experimental farms, movies, and other summer tourist attractions. She has shown me many neat science experiments at home that she has done with her high school students. She has also taught me how to play tennis and basketball and has given me lots of camping tips.

Aunt Sherry is my hero because she loves me and cares for me like a son and a best friend. She means the world to me.

Mitchell Bond

Abraham Goldfarb

You may think that all heroes have to have a secret lair. Well, my hero doesn't. He has a condominium in Toronto and works for a plumbing company. My hero is my zaideh (grandfather). My family is Jewish and a lot of my family was in Poland during World War 2, including my zaideh. He saved half of my family. He traveled from Poland to Russia to Belgium to Canada. He was also a lumberjack in Russia, to escape the Nazis.

I wouldn't be alive today if Zaideh didn't say "Hitler's crazy, I'm getting out of here." My great bubby (grandmother) said, "You're too young to go." My zaideh said, "Well, I'm not staying here." His mother and father said, "Then we'll have to go with you." If he hadn't been so strong about leaving, my dad, my sister, my two brothers, my uncle and his four children, my cousin, Toby, and her two children, her brother, Abe, and his four children, would have never been born.

Even though he was only 18, he took a train from Poland to Russia and it was not easy to do. Things were so bad in Russia that he was ready to go back to Poland. Instead, the Russians sent him north almost all the way to the Arctic Circle, where he worked for five years as a lumberjack until the war ended. After the war, the Russians let him and his family leave Russia. There was nothing left to go to in Poland, so he went with his family to Belgium for three years, while he waited for a visa to Canada. After he came to Canada, he put himself through school to become a plumber.

My zaideh, Abraham Goldfarb, saved half of my family, he traveled across three continents and he was a lumberjack in Russia. He is also a great zaideh and I love him very much.

Eli Goldfarb

Sandra Bloomberg

When my cousin, Sandi, was born, everything seemed normal. When she was born, she had a mom and a dad and a big brother who all loved her very much. Things started to unravel when her parents found out she had juvenile diabetes. Every day, her urine had to be tested for sugar and she had to be given an insulin injection. She was not allowed to eat food with sugar in it, like all of her friends.

The next bad thing happened in her life when she was still in elementary school (only nine years old) and her mom died of cancer. When Sandi was 18, she moved in with an elderly lady named Mrs. Kaiman. While she was living with Mrs. Kaiman, she worked at the university bookstore to pay her rent and to pay her tuition.

Sandi graduated from university and worked as a bank teller. She became engaged to a man who left her because of her diabetes. She then was in a car accident and became blind in one eye. Soon after that, her brother developed schizophrenia. Sandi did her best to take as much care of him as possible, but it was not easy.

Sandi married a man and felt very lucky. In the summer of 2004, Sandi had to have her leg removed because of diabetes. Once Sandi learned to walk on her artificial leg, she wanted to learn how to skate on it. Because of diabetes, she died in October 2004, at the age of 47.

Sandi had amazing friends and a husband who loved her. She never felt sorry for herself. She was kind and happy to be alive and grateful for what she had.

Jacob Goldfarb

Cameron Graham

My dad followed his dream to have a sports store. The entire family has contributed time to the store and lots of people in the community shop at my dad's store because they get good service and they trust him. My dad's store is called Just Sports, By Cam. I believe my dad's store will be very successful.

My dad is always there for me. When I need him because of problems at school, he always comes. He teaches me sports and helps me play them. We both like hockey and football and we play them together.

My dad never gives up on his dreams. He is confident in himself. He is still trying to win NHL '06 on the PS2 (because he never wins). He never gave up on his dream of having a family - he worked hard to adopt me. That makes my bond with my dad very special.

Karac Graham

Mrs. (Martha) Attema

Mrs. Attema, my grade one teacher, feels most comfortable in jeans and a t-shirt. She is my hero because of her commitment to reducing energy consumption, writing and teaching.

Mrs. Attema is committed to reducing energy consumption. She has a straw bale house, solar panels and a Smart car. She also has a wind turbine to produce electricity for her home.

She is also an author. I love to read Mrs. Attema's books. I have read The Paper Wagon and Hero. She inspired me to read and write. Mrs. Attema holds a writing club at my school. I was in her writing club for three years where we learned to write stories, poems and different kinds of riddles.

Another reason Mrs. Attema is special is that she is a grade one teacher at Vincent Massey Public School. She has taught for many years. She is a kind teacher.

Sydney Graham

Todd Gribbon

My hero is my dad. Dad went through the hard death of his father at the age of 14. His little brother, Scott, was seven and his older brother, Grant, was 15 when their father died. My grandfather was in a car accident when he passed away. He was going to get gas for the ski-doo and another man hit him with his truck. My dad had to help his mother with doing chores around the house. They were chores that most teenagers wouldn't do. My dad has been without his father for a long time.

My dad is my hero because he is accomplished. He set a goal in life to be a teacher. He has been to many places and always sets goals. He reached his goal of being a teacher even though school wasn't his thing. My dad has a learning disability but he keeps on learning the way he needs to learn, by trying, doing and trying again. Now he is Vice-Principal at West Ferris Secondary School and wants to be a principal.

My dad also helps me in all different ways. He helps me set goals in areas where I have difficulties. He teaches me how to play sports better, like helping me with my foot skills in soccer, setting in volleyball or playing squash. He also helps me with my school work and be a better person. He pushes me and expects me to do my best in anything that I try in life. He is my hero and I love him a lot.

Kathryn Gribbon

Dave Hargrave

My dad is Dave Hargrave. He is a good dad and he is not too busy to play. However, it was not always that way.

In March of 1980, my dad joined the military. He went to Cornwall for his basic training. Cornwall is in Nova Scotia. The training lasted for 13 weeks. In Cornwall, they taught him how to march. They also taught him about health and fitness, military history, and the importance of teamwork. When this was finished, he went to Wainright, Alberta, for four months of infantry training where he learned how to maintain and care for equipment such as radios, tents, boots, rifles, and pistols. They practiced with dummy rounds and dummy grenades. Dummy means they are not live and cannot hurt someone. Then they went on live fire exercises. All this training resulted in a well-disciplined fighting force.

During this time, he also learned how to throw grenades. The practice grenades didn't explode. The types of guns he learned to use were a semi-automatic rifle, a machine gun, and a pistol. I don't know how I feel about this. It was very shocking. Over the years he learned to use other weapons.

When training was finished, my dad was sent to the Princess Patricia Canadian Light Infantry in Calgary. This was where his home would be. While living in Calgary, my dad learned how to drive tanks. They can also be called armour personnel carriers.

While on course in Edmonton, he met my mom, Sarah. They were introduced on a blind date. They moved east to Trenton, Ontario. During the first Gulf War, he was in Germany sending supplies to the war. In 1992 and 1993, he flew humanitarian supplies into Russia. That was very exciting and cool. Dad and Mom have four kids: Corrine, Kevin, Brandon and me, Tyler. In the 90's, he flew supplies in Sarajevo. He loaded the planes in Italy and flew them to Sarajevo, landed, and unloaded. All the time, the enemy was shooting at the plane.

In 1996, my dad was posted to North Bay. The day the moving trucks came to move us out, my mom and dad went to the hospital in Belleville because I was being born. That day was August 3rd, 1996.

In North Bay, my dad worked in base traffic. He was controlling moving companies in North Bay and Northern Ontario. This was a good time because my dad was home more often. He would play baseball, ball tag, and everything. All the kids would always ask if my dad could come out and play, too. But then, my dad got Parkinson's and was forced to retire from the military. My dad is in pain a lot, but no matter what, he always finds time to play with me. When he feels good, we go bike riding and play ball and other sports stuff at the field. He plays board games and cards with me, too.

Tyler Hargrave

Lou Valenti

My great uncle Lou was brave because he made it through World War II, he was loyal because he came and visited us, and he was kind because he told me stories.

My great uncle Lou fought in World War II. He had to face a lot of death near the end of the war. He got shot in the back and he got sent home. He was also brave because he had cancer and he fought it for a long time.

Not only was he brave but he was a loyal friend. He came to my house on every holiday, even when he had cancer. Even though he was sick, he never stopped loving us and we never stopped loving him.

He was a loyal friend and kind. He told me stories about World War II. He came over to my house because he loved us a lot. My great uncle Lou was very caring.

John Knox

Andrew Bubarh

Andrew Bubarh is a normal 21-year-old who wants to make a difference. Have you ever been to Africa? Well, Andrew has. He went because he is promoting black and white people to interact with each other better.

He also helps out at the university by building a solar-powered bus shelter, helps international students, and organizes a festival to promote recycling and Frisbee games.

Being in Africa inspired him to send more people there. He is now raising money to send more people to build clean water filters and build houses and to bring environmentally friendly coffee.

Andrew has made a difference in the world and wants to inspire more people to do the same.

Evan Lechlitner

Carolyn Keene

I'm Kristen Zamperoni. If you know me you probably know that I love to read! Carolyn Keene writes my favorite series of books. If you guessed mystery and the Nancy Drew series, you're right! I think the Nancy Drew series she writes has the best thrills, cliffhangers and titles.

The thrills in Carolyn Keene's books are like when Nancy's just about to solve a mystery and something in the story twists and Nancy is looking for more clues. The other kinds of thrills are when Nancy finds the person who did the crime but it's not the person she thought. There are still many more thrills in her books like surprise injuries, or all of a sudden, Nancy needs help. Another is when her father is kidnapped and Nancy finds mysterious clues that lead her off track of solving the mystery!

Carolyn Keene can easily write cliffhangers. She also has amazing titles that make you want to read on. Here are three examples: The Secret of the Old Clock, The Hidden Staircase and The Bungalow Mystery. Don't you think those titles are amazing? I don't know about you, but I can't come up with titles like that!

I'm Kristen Zamperoni and I love to read! Now you know why Carolyn Keene is my hero! She is my hero because of the thrills, cliffhangers and her really good titles. Don't you just want to read her books now?

Kristen Zamperoni

Hero Highlights From Our Terrific Threes & Fantastic Fours

Stacey Lynn Melrose

"Sometimes, my hero wears pajamas or jeans, but a lot of the time she wears combats. Her name is Stacy Lynn Melrose, but I call her Mom. My mother is very special to me because she has three jobs. She was a single parent to me and my brother for a very long time, she helps me with my homework and she is in the military, helping in North Bay and in Afghanistan."

Anastasia Amos

Brian Bowes

"I have a friend with friendship bigger than a blue whale. He is my dad. My dad is my hero because he is happy, funny, and there for me. I can do things with my dad. You don't look at the newspaper when talking to him. You look at the man who's there when you want him to be there."

Mike Bowes

Jon Marcil

"Mr. Marcil recycles more than anyone I know because he runs the recycling depot. He helps the environment by stopping pollution. Even though he works with garbage, he doesn't smell bad. That's why Jon Marcil is my hero and if you knew what I know, he'd be your hero, too."

Cameron Cole

Laurie Daniels

Not only did my Auntie Laurie care for people, but she was a very giving person as well. She gave away the old toys and clothes she didn't use anymore. But, according to my Auntie Laurie, the word "giving" didn't just mean to give away old clothes and toys. To her, it meant to love other people and be kind to them and that is what she did.

Lauren Daniels

Fred Culin

"Even though my grandpa Fred owns a business, he loves to fly his plane. He still does all those things, even though he is a little bit old. He takes Young Eagles in his plane for a ride. This is all done by volunteering. He takes no money. He takes me for rides in his plane. When you lift off the lake, you can clearly see people biking, walking, driving, and swimming. The plane is small, but big enough to hold my grandpa, dad, and ...me! I'm glad to call him my grandpa."

Matthew Culin

Harold Fennell

"My grandpa Harold is kind, caring, and special to me. He is no longer alive. He made horses for the waterfront carousel, so I guess he taught me how to paint. He also taught me how to read because when I was little, he would take me away and read me a book. He used different voices for different characters. It made us laugh. Each of us would sit on one knee, me on one side and TJ on the other. My grandpa was a great storyteller."

Jody Fennell

Kevin Hawton

"My dad is raising three very talented and successful children. He tries his best to make them happy and to get to all of their activities. We may not be the most perfect little angels, but my dad sure cleans up after us."

Emily Hawton

Sgt. Jim Lennips

"My dad helps me build things like Lego towers, castles, and forts. He helped me build a musical instrument for school. It was a stringed guitar made out of wood. My dad is a fabulous hero because we do things together. He takes me places where he and I want to go. He helps people when he is doing his job."

J.L.L.

Kathryn MacLellan

"My mom, Kathryn, is a great teacher for me and other kids. My mom has taught me lots of things since I was born, like how to talk and walk and even how to ride a bike. My mom teaches me how to use my manners. She even helps teach me school work. My mom's job is a teacher and she helps other kids at our school. I've learned a lot from my mom and I will keep learning from her."

Jillian MacLellan

Eileen Larmer

"When my nana Eileen was 67 years old, she was diagnosed with cancer in the muscle of her left leg. It was the same cancer that killed Terry Fox. She has had five operations to her leg but she has been left with a broken leg that will never heal. My nana is doing fine. She walks on her leg every day, with a crutch. The treatments have made my nana very tired but she still comes for visits and makes me her delicious chocolate chip cookies. Most of all, my nana never complains and gives me so much love."

Noah Perron

Theresa Moran

"My grandma Theresa is very brave because she is battling cancer and has an amazing attitude. Her cancer began years ago and then it went away. It came back last year in her breast. It spread to her liver and her bones. Just when it was beginning to be under control, it spread to her brain. Through it all, she has remained positive. She is a fighter and she never gives up."

Madison Tranter

Donald Willis

My dad is strong in mind and body. I think this, even though he can't lift up a building and jump over a mountain at the same time. He can lift up a table and jump over a medium-sized rock to help people move furniture. Also, I think he is quick to think things like 67 x 35 on his feet.

Mackenzie Willis

Jessie Johnson

"Jessie is caring. If I am bleeding, Jessie will give me a Band-aid. Sometimes he lets me use his toys and sometimes he lets me have Pokemon cards. He waits for me if I have to go to the washroom, or if I have to get something. Jessie listens to what I have to say. Jessie is talented because he can do 50 hops on his pogo and he says it's really hard. I can only do up to five hops."

Jacob Meldrum

CHAPTER FOURTEEN

OUR COMMUNITY

How wonderful it is that nobody need wait a single moment before starting to improve the world.

Anne Frank

Ava Vosu

Like many women from my generation, I worked for several years before deciding to start a family. The news of my pregnancy was met with both anticipation and trepidation. Would I be able to create a healthy baby? Was I cut out for the job of motherhood? What were my options for delivering the baby? So many questions, so much self-doubt. It's one thing to take care of yourself, but the thought of bringing a new life into the world added so much anxiety about my capability.

A friend referred me to local midwife, Ava Vosu. My partner, Dave, was skeptical of the midwifery process but I convinced him to attend a consult. After learning more about Ava's experience with over 600 births at that time, we were confident in her care.

The journey began toward motherhood. The growing life inside me presented a multitude of questions. I found myself contacting the clinic in Powassan constantly. Can I eat this, can I do that, can I stand on my head...most of them silly as I look back. Ava and her staff always met my curiosity with time to talk, resources to take home and read or watch, and a calm sense of caring, humour, and confidence-building. Throughout the pregnancy, Ava referred me to other women practitioners in the community: Dr. Cindy Stewart for chiropractics, Jeannie Mackay with a unique method of healing, Dana Monette for life-altering "massage therapy" work, homeopathic and naturopathic healers and others.

After the home birth of my first baby, a healthy boy, Ava's nursing attendant, Anne Smith, said to me, "Doesn't this experience really change the way we perceive ourselves as women?" I will never forget these words or the experience of delivering a beautiful baby in our home. I felt powerful, capable, grateful, confident and most of all, at one with nature.

The experience of meeting Ava and her network of natural healers changed my life. They taught me about health, they taught me about surrendering to nature, and they taught me that health and nature are one force. Believing in myself and my abilities to create and maintain optimum health for myself and my baby was the important focus at this time. Most importantly, I was able to bring my children into the world in a loving and welcoming environment.

As an advocate of natural birth, Ava has worked diligently throughout her career to promote practices and choices that women have while pregnant and delivering their babies. Her life-long career focus has been "to ensure the rights of birthing women". In 1981, Ava formed the Association of Ontario Midwifery, with a mission to have the practice recognized. As a result, our government now officially recognizes midwifery as an option for women. When a professional advocates and gains the right for people to choose, they are heroes and many people benefit.

Now with two beautiful children brought into the world in a peaceful, healthy, loving environment, I am forever grateful to Ava for her dedication to the profession of midwifery, and the progress that she has made for the benefit of women in our community. This experience has had a major impact on my life.

Penny Tremblay
Mother of two

* It is noted that Marsha (nee Elkhorn), who started the North Bay Transition House for women, had a great deal of influence over Ava as a neighbour during Ava's childhood. Ava's interest in midwifery was inspired by Marsha as she witnessed her first breastfeeding mother.

Molly Penny

When I was six years old, I had a kind of cancer that was very rare to girls called Burkits Lymphoma. A nice lady named Molly Penny would come to the hospital room to make me, and all of the other children, very happy. I was cured of cancer when I was about eight years old. I still had to go for check-ups and Molly Penny would still come up to see me. All of the doctors would try to cheer me up, but Molly Penny was the only one who could get me that happy.

Molly Penny became my hero during the times when I didn't know where I belonged. I never really fit in with all the other kids. Then, Molly Penny helped me understand who I really am, inside of my heart. She told me, "Ashley, you are a special little girl. You just don't know that yet. You know who you are, but you just need to follow your heart to find yourself."

I didn't know how much my friends cared about me but when they sent me all kinds of loving and caring letters and messages on my mom's video camera, I finally understood all the things that Molly Penny was telling me.

Ashley Robinson, 11

Editor's Note: Molly Penny's real name is Ruth Collins. She is a nurse at the Children's Hospital of Eastern Ontario, in Ottawa. To cheer up the children, she dresses as a clown and the clown's name is Molly Penny.

A Lucky Baby Deer

Every baby is beautiful, especially when they`re only a few days old. The first time I saw her lying in bed, no bigger than a dinner plate and looking up at me with her big, blue eyes, I felt no different. She was the most beautiful thing in the entire world and I couldn`t imagine loving anyone so much, so quickly. She stole my heart with her adorable, soft, black nose, her long, spindly legs, and her soft, spotted coat. Oh, and did I mention she was a deer?

This little creature I`m talking about is named Lucky. Her story is an uncommon one, to say the least. Unlike most baby deer that are raised in the wild, Lucky had a whole neighbourhood to rely on for love, care and nurturing. Never before has such a small animal had such a strong impact on people`s lives.

Lucky was found at only a few hours old, hiding in a patch of daisies. Her mother had been hit and killed by a car. Luckily for her, a man named Jim found her and took her home to his wife, Brenda. I wasn`t introduced to Big J and Brenda until a few days after they brought Lucky home. Little did we know how much she would eventually mean to all of us. At the time, although I didn`t know it, Brenda was fighting ovarian cancer for the second time. The appearance of Lucky meant a welcome distraction, a new baby to focus on, and a postive place to direct everyone`s attention.

This spotted miracle took our neighbourhood by storm. Everyone wanted to see her and to be a part of her upbringing. Neighbours would stop by, daily, to bring our fawn some sort of little treat; freshly picked strawberries or honey from their beehives. Other times, they would come just for the company, to talk with the loving couple that had taken Lucky in, and to play a quick game of hide and seek in the flowerbeds with the little deer. It wasn't long before all of Brenda's potted plants were bare and her garden was covered in hoof prints. There were never any complaints, though. Lucky had the most amazing way of taking hold of your heart with just a glance. It would start with a large Corona-bottle full of milk in your hands, as she pawed at your legs in bliss, and, from that moment on, there was no turning back.

It wasn't just our neighbourhood, either. People came to see her from all over Ontario and even a few from the States. I once heard that her picture had made it over to Afghanistan and was spreading her love amongst our soldiers there. Lucky's name ended up being to her benefit as she was struck by a car once, and had to have her front leg put in a cast. News spread fast and, once again, the compassion and strength of our neighbourhood came out. A doctor in Barrie, who was a friend of a friend of Lucky's, even offered to install a metal plate in her leg, if it came down to that. Luckily for Lucky, the work of two local vets proved to be all that she needed.

Adding to this, Lucky's new mother was not doing well. Brenda's health was starting to turn. Although Lucky had not entered the house in months, she reverted to pawing at the patio door to be let in, several times a day. This only happened once Brenda grew too uncomfortable to move around and enjoy the outdoors as often as she used to. Despite the independence and fondness for exploring that our growing deer was experiencing, she was never far from home.

A favorite but sad story of Big J's and the neighbourhood is of the day Brenda entered the hospital for the last time. It was less than a week before Brenda's birthday and we had all hoped she would last long enough to celebrate with us. Instead, the ambulances were called and the neighbourhood reacted with cautious despair. As the story goes, Lucky pushed her way between two paramedics to lick Brenda's face one last time. With tears in their eyes, everyone knew that there was no way they were taking her away without a goodbye from her baby. The experience was a first for the paramedics, as she brought so many firsts for many of us.

Lucky's life has by no means been easy. She was orphaned at just a few days old, lost her adopted mother, Brenda, to cancer, and was struck by a car the following fall. Even with these odds against her, she managed to do more for our neighbourhood than most people do in their whole lives. She brought many people together with a strange but enduring love and left her impression on anyone who knew her or even just knew of her. She has loved us all unconditionally and continues to do so from her new home in Huntsville.

Amanda Jewell, 17

Phyllis Bell
(A Second Chance)

On April 5, 1984, I was asleep in my townhouse on Lakeshore Drive. My son, Alex, who was almost three at the time, got out of his bed at 4 a.m. and came into my room to wake me up. I got out of bed and picked him up in my arms. I asked him what was wrong...his head fell backwards as if he was very sick.

Phyllis Bell, our next door neighbour, babysat my son when my wife was at Canadore and I was working at Fabrene. I called Phyllis at 4 a.m. and asked her to come over because I did not know what was wrong with my son. After about 10 minutes, she hadn't shown up yet. I carried my son to the front door and looked out to see if Phyllis was coming. I didn't see her yet but I could smell something hot...maybe the stove was on. I checked and it was off.

I left my son on the living room floor and went down to the basement. Next to the basement is the garage. When I opened the doorway to the garage, I could almost chew the smoke, it was so thick. Our car was running inside the garage and I found my wife on the floor on the opposite side of the car. I lifted up the garage door and dragged her out onto the driveway. It was a crappy night. It was raining. I put my hand over her eyes to see if her pupils had movement. They did not. I gave her artificial respiration until Phyllis showed up.

Phyllis said, "Bob, shut off the car. Where's Alex?" I shut off the car. "In the living room," I said, and went back in through the garage. I opened the door to the rec room and fell down as I went in, hitting my head on the edge of an electric baseboard heater. I got back up and I went up the basement stairs to the living room with Phyllis pushing me from behind. The next thing I knew, I was sitting in the driveway clearing my head.

Phyllis got my son out and he was revived in the ambulance. There's more to this story, but I want to thank Phyllis from the bottom of my heart for saving my life and the life of my son, Alex, and for giving us a second chance.

Robert W. Moore

Lynne Roy

My hero is Lynne. Lynne is cool and awesome. She helps Sarah, Martha and David. I like how she helps Sarah with blocks. She feeds Martha dessert and takes Sarah for walks.

Lynne lets me watch movies and listen to my music. Lynne is beautiful. She does not argue. She tells me I'm a good boy. I like how she says, "Good job, David! I'm so proud of you!" Lynne is my friend.

David Olivier

Editor's Note: Lynne is a respite worker working with David. David is a Grade 10 student at West Ferris Secondary School.

Chriss Wagner

I met you, oh, maybe 10 years ago. You had just moved to North Bay with your husband, who had been transferred with his company. We were at the curling rink, in the mixed league, and became fast friends. One night, I needed a ride home and - lo and behold - we lived on the same street. I said, "Be careful, the Clampetts (from the show Beverley Hillbillies) have moved into your neighbourhood." A few years later, I also jokingly noted that their property value not only went down with the Clampetts on their street, but that they lived on a fault line, after we had the earthquake on January 1, 2000. Before the big quake, Chriss and I would get together, on occasion, to share a bottle of wine or go for a walk and chat.

She was an amazing mother. With her first marriage, she had a daughter and then, soon after, twin girls; the family grew fast. Chriss divorced and found the love of her life in a new gentleman named Greg. He was divorced with two small children, a boy and girl, who were a bit younger than Chriss' girls. What a great family: Chriss and Greg, with five children. Being great parents, they went on to have two more boys together. Braxton was first and Keegan came next.

While I was not a part of their lives at that time, I heard a bit of the story. Just after two years of age, Braxton showed symptoms of Mitochondria Myopia, a very rare, genetic disease, and was hospitalized in a children's hospital down south. For almost a year, Chriss traveled every day to the hospital, over an hour each way, while raising six other children. God bless Greg for working and caring for the family during this trying time. Braxton spent almost a year in the children's hospital with a respirator and feeding tube. Chriss finally demanded that the hospital show her how to care for him at home since she had other children to care for.

Chriss and Greg turned their living room into a hospital room for Braxton. One day shortly thereafter, Keegan came down with symptoms as well. The doctors said that Keegan was showing the same signs of the very rare disease. Not wanting to put Keegan through the same hospitalization as Braxton, with the feeding tube and ventilator, Chriss and Greg decided to keep Keegan at home. He died peacefully a few weeks later. Yes, having to tell family and friends that Keegan had passed away, at age two, was difficult. Most said, "No, you must mean Braxton", and the answer was no - "We are speaking of Keegan". They had lost a child. No one should ever lose a child! I believe it was approximately seven weeks later that Braxton, at age three, was laid to rest beside his brother. God bless the whole family for moving on and living their lives while they remember their two beautiful, happy boys, who filled their lives with such joy for such a short time.

This is my story of my friend. She is a wonderful person. Her whole family should be commended for moving forward with their lives. As a mother myself, I appreciate Chriss' strength and commitment to ensure that her other children were well cared for and brought up in this world to carry on. She also raised a niece who was in need. She is now a grandmother of six. To this day, she loves her husband and five children dearly. They have lives to live and contributions to make to the future. God bless their family and their strength.

Patti Carr

Danielle Trudeau and Paige Shemilt

My name is Victoria and I am nine years old. I have not made many friends yet as I am quite shy and I have a learning disability. Mommy started taking me to Oxford to help me learn and I have met two of the nicest people in the world; Danielle Trudeau and her daughter, Paige Shemilt. They are both my heroes. Danielle has helped me learn so that I can keep up with my classmates. I never liked going to school because the kids would make fun of me and would not want to play with me. Danielle has taught me how to work with my disability and has accepted me the way I am. I don't feel different with her; I feel like everyone else. She has become my friend too. She is very kind and gentle, not only with me but also with the other students at the centre. Danielle makes learning fun. I love her very much and will always be her friend.

Paige is 15 and she also treats me like a friend. She is going to show me how to play volleyball. She is a really good player. Sometimes we go to the movies and to dinner and she even let me walk her new puppy, Lily. Paige is also my best friend; I love her a lot too. When I grow up, I want to be just like her. Paige has a lot of friends her own age but she still manages to take time out of her busy schedule for me. Paige goes to high school, works, takes music lessons, plays volleyball, and helps Danielle at the centre. Everyone loves her. She is also so kind and funny. She makes me laugh. I enjoy every moment we spend together. With both Paige and Danielle as my friends,

I don't feel as lonely anymore and I am starting to make new friends at school because they have given me the confidence in myself to overcome my shyness. In a way, both Paige and Danielle have saved my life as I did not think I would ever have friends; now I have two of the best. I will always love my two heroes.

Victoria Cook, 9

P.S. I do not know how to write stories yet, but I wanted you to know how I felt about my heroes.

Editor's Note: Victoria, our editor's disagree with your post script comment. We happen to think you can write quite well! :o)

Chantalle Battiston

We all have dreams, fantasies and goals. I was diagnosed with high depression and was at the point where I didn't even leave my room. Counseling was done at home and different medications were tried every week. Nothing was helping and by that point, I was starting high school with no hopes, no dreams. Nothing.

If anything, I wanted to die. High school seemed to only make things worse and, before I knew it, I was back at the doctor's and was being diagnosed with acute anxiety. My anxiety increased as the days went on and it seemed to sky-rocket by the hour. I was pulled out of school in late November and I realized I was home-bound. I never left, not even to go to the corner store. I was so terrified and of what, I couldn't tell you.

Agoraphobia is not an easy phobia to conquer. A year went by and life seemed short-handed. I sat in my room and wrote. That was my life. So many different thoughts were running through my head, as fast as they could go. There wasn't even time to stop and think about a certain one. Will I get better? How can I live like this? The day that I met Chantalle Battiston changed my life completely.

Consider, for yourself, what it would be like to see a therapist that you know nothing about and who looks the same age as you. You can probably imagine the first few thoughts that ran through my mind, "I can counsel this lady! She can't possibly help me!" I was wrong. I saw Chantalle twice, for an hour each time and, after the second session, I left my house! I went out for the first time in two years. I couldn't believe it. This lady was a miracle and this was a life-altering change.

From that day on, everything has just kept rolling. I've been seeing Chantalle for five months now and I'm barely ever home. It's amazing! I have my life back. I thank my friends and family for supporting me through all of this. Chantalle, you are my hero!

Marley Anne Caley, 16

Lori-Ann Coffin
(Sea-Swept Teddy Bear)

My hero is Lori-Ann Coffin, a close family friend and the only one who was brave enough to save my teddy bear. I haven't talked to her in awhile, but I'll never forget what happened that day.

When I was little, about five or so, my parents and my brother and I all lived out in the bush, right on the lake. My parents had been in the market for a new boat and had rented a pontoon boat just for fun. When they asked our neighbours in the cottage next to our place to come with us, they said yes. So Lori-Ann, her mom, dad, and brother all came along for the ride.

The wind was blowing fiercely that day. The water was quite chilly. I sat on the floor of the boat while all the big people got the seats. My teddy bear, Lumpy, and I were content with playing on the floor. We were about a hundred feet away from the dock when a gust of wind stole Lumpy from my hands and tossed him into the lake. Being a little girl with my bear slowly fading away, I began to panic and cry. My dad shut off the motor and everyone on the boat tried to grab Lumpy before he got too far away, or sunk, because they all knew how much I loved him. Their attempts were unsuccessful.

Then, taking it upon herself, Lori-Ann stripped down to her bathing suit and dove into the lake. She saved my bear and was back on the boat in less than a minute. Right then, I was probably the most grateful, happiest little girl on earth.

I still have Lumpy today, though he's not nearly as cute or as white as he was back then. Without Lori-Ann, my bear would have sunk and I would have been crushed.

Dana McCrea

Cliff Noth
(A Real Titan)

"We're going to make a swimmer out of you yet". These are the words that encourage me to push a little harder on that last 25 metres or kick a little harder during tough sprints. They have made me love swimming, not because I want to become an Olympic athlete, but because I want to have fun and stay healthy. They have made me believe in myself and challenge myself to do better. These are the words of Cliff Noth, my coach.

I joined the North Bay Y Titans Swim Team this September, having no idea what to expect and having practically no background in the sport. I took swimming lessons when I was a kid, whereas everyone else on the team had been swimming competitively since they were six. All I had going in were a couple of friends who were already on the team and the assurance that swimming was the 'sweetest sport ever'.

My first week on the team, I almost drowned on numerous occasions while trying to learn butterfly. I was always last in my group by far and I felt like I belonged in the pool about as much as a fish on land. But every time I missed a 50-metre because I was too far behind the rest of the group or came out of the water panting, Cliff was there to tell me that I was doing great and to remind me that it's ok to be a little behind. When some of the sets were too hard for me, he would tweak them a little to make sure I would have a chance at making the times. When I missed practices, I was welcomed back to the pool by the team and I could count on a joke or two from Cliff. He made sure I was comfortable and tried to give me tips and advice on how to improve my technique.

At my first swim meet in Sudbury, I was completely terrified because I had never raced before and I still was not that fast. Cliff did not put any pressure on me to perform; he would just tell me to have fun with it and 'let her rip" before every race.

He has been an amazing coach. If you are slacking, he will tell you to pick up the pace. If you are doing well, he will tell you that you are doing awesome and to keep doing what you're doing. He treats everyone the same no matter how young, how fast, or how many practices they attend in a week. Whether you win or lose, laugh or cry, he's there to support you and make sure you are having fun. Cliff makes sure that there is a positive environment on deck and that he has a chance to laugh and chat with the team a bit before each practice. Whether it is telling us a story about something that happened in the swim world, or talking about bowel movements, he makes sure everyone is included.

He is there to teach us to be better swimmers but, at the same time, he wants to teach us to be better people outside the pool. I have learned so much about myself during my time on the team. My confidence and self-esteem have grown so much and I have become much more self-assured. Cliff was there to help me see my potential as an athlete and as a person. From me and the rest of the team - thank you - for being a role model and an amazing coach.

Sonia Kaminski-Morneault, 17

Linda Beatty

This is my story of Linda Beatty, who works at the Red Cross. Linda was my bath lady, coming over every Friday morning at 8 a.m. This went on for almost a year.

One Friday, Linda came to give me my bath. The door was unlocked. Linda would come in and go upstairs as my bathroom was up there. I slept in the rec room due to my condition from a cancer operation. When Linda did not hear from me, she came down to the rec room to find me in a diabetic coma. She got my wife and brought her downstairs from the second floor. Linda called the ambulance and they found that my diabetic count was down to one.

By noon, I would have been dead if I had not gotten the care of the ambulance attendants. Linda saved my life by calling the ambulance when she did. I called Linda 'my saviour' from then on.

Rod Moore

CHAPTER FIFTEEN

OUR
HERO WITHIN

*Why should I care what other people
think of me? I am who I am. And who
I wanna be.*

Avril Lavigne

.

Mikayla Werner

I'd love to tell you I have heroes. I'd like to admit that my parents were great role models. I'd like nothing more than to go on and on about how wonderful my life is because of them. I should be able to tell you there is no suicide note behind the picture of Jesus sitting on the dresser, or that my father was always coming to pick me up for all the weekend visits he was allotted after the messy divorce. I wish I could tell you that my father was my hero because he valued me at the same level as his new wife, but that's not the case. Don't get me wrong. I'm not asking for sympathy and I'd prefer it if you didn't read this at all. But now that you've begun, I might as well continue. We both know that once the reader has been exposed to something tragic, he cannot stop reading it until there is catharsis....

Honestly, I would like to write about someone important enough to be my hero. In fact, I approached writing this with the hopes of finding a role model or hero. I suppose I could use my imaginary friend, who stuck with me through the years of mental abuse until about grade seven, but that would point out that I was late to develop in social skills and that I never invited anyone to play with me after school. But if you were to ask me what a hero is, I would tell you a hero is someone who saves. A hero has the ability to save someone, or something, from an awful fate and chooses to do so.

If I wanted to, I could tell you that the man I fell in love with, at age 17, was a hero to me. I could tell you that he opened my eyes to what was going on around me and pulled me out of the grave of guilt that I had carved for myself. If my life were darkness, he was my ray of light. So, yeah, I guess I have a hero; he saved me in more ways than one.

'Well, what about your friends?' you ask. My friends have come and gone and although I would never speak of it to them, I am used to leaving people behind. There are so many scars etched into my heart from people who have touched it ever so slightly over the years and they sink deeper the farther away I move. The sad thing is, I cannot remember half of their names. Their faces rise to the surface of my mind every now and again, to remind me I had people to look out for at my other schools. If they were heroes of mine when I was younger, I'm certain they helped shape me into who I am today, however faded my memory of them.

My school teachers are heroes of mine, I suppose. They were the ones who honed the art of patience and used it on me when I was having a hard time adjusting to a new school, or new classes in the middle of a semester. They inspired me and kept me on the right path (although homework was a concept that took me a lot longer to grasp). I could tell you I graduated because of them and I have a future in this brave, new world because of that.

But if you asked me to pinpoint one specific hero, I'd tell you that there is not one person who could hold the weight I do. Surely they would be crushed under the events of my life and that is a fate I wouldn't wish upon anyone. If you were to look at it from my point of view, I am my own hero. After all, I've done pretty well for myself, haven't I? You see, despite the many unfavorable things that have happened, I survived. I'm doing pretty well for myself, I might add. And now I'm here to tell you that it's okay to lean on yourself every once in a while. When there is no one else to save you, sometimes you have to be your own hero.

Mikayla Werner

THANK YOU
FOR READING OUR BOOK.

We hope you have enjoyed the stories of our local heroes.

We have a GIFT for you...

**Our sponsors have given generously to this cause
so that we could donate $8.00 - $10.00 of
every book sold to local charities.**

The next section of the book is dedicated to our
sponsors. As a THANK YOU to the sponsors, please take
a moment to read through their ads. Next time you are out
and about in the community, take a moment to stop by
their place of business and say,
"I saw your ad in the You're My Hero™ book - Thanks!"

HERE IS OUR GIFT OFFER TO YOU.

Simply take a few minutes to answer the questions in the
SPONSOR QUIZ

(see next page)

E-mail your answers to: quiz@ymhbooks.com

We will send you a FREE e-copy of an interview that
Barry Spilchuk did with Jack Canfield of
Chicken Soup for the Soul®.

**Jack discusses - Sudden Wealth - How to create an
in-flow of money and how to manage and protect it.**

SPONSOR QUIZ
GIFT OFFER

E-mail us the answers to these 10 questions and we will send you a **FREE** e-copy of an interview that Barry Spilchuk did with Jack Canfield - founder of Chicken Soup for the Soul®.

E-mail your answers to: quiz@ymhbooks.com

1) In the ad for CALLANDER BAY DENTAL CENTER - How much money did they raise for charity in 2007?

2) In the ad for JACK LOCKHART ART GALLERY - What is the object that he has placed his wording on?

3) How many miners are pictured in the CEMENTATION ad?

4) Who is the person pictured in the ad for CALLANDER BAY REAL ESTATE?

5) In the BEST WESTERN ad - Name two things in the picture on the bottom right.

6) In the ad for ALLISON THE BOOKMAN - What are the addresses for their two locations?

7) In the FAITHFUL PRINTS ad - What is their web address?

8) CAISSE POPULAIRE pictures a young child in their ad - What is the child wearing on her face?

9) How many North Bay locations are listed on the EUPHORIA SMOOTHIES ad?

10) What are the people doing in the ad for CHIRO PARTNERS?

Photo by Graeme Oxby

Everyday Heroes

Cementation is proud to be the first company to sponsor the *You're My Hero* project in North Bay. In our company we have many employees who exercise courageous leadership in safety. These employees are our everyday heroes because by promoting safe work practices they prevent injuries and ultimately save lives, and what could be more heroic than that.

We believe in everyday heroes.

EUPHORIC ACTS OF KINDNESS
SMOOTHIE KARMA

Purchase a Smoothie Karma Certificate that will allow Euphoria to offer a free smoothie to random customers. You can also hand-out a Smoothie Karma certificate randomly. Euphoria stores will offer a Smoothie Karma certificate to two customers per day . . . and so the ripple will grow!

Euphoria and You're My Hero™ Books Ltd.
are giving you your next regular Euphoria Smoothie as an act of euphoric kindness.
Feels nice doesn't it? You can multiply that feeling by "paying it forward" and buying a smoothie for someone else. You're it. Pass it on: anonymously make someone smile and keep the smoothie karma going!
(find the detachable certificate inserted in this book)

Kindness is contagious.
Euphoria is dedicated to small acts of kindness.
Thank you for being Euphoric!

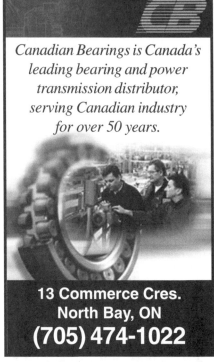

Peter McKeown, Rick Doughty & all the staff at ROGERS Radio

would like to salute all the heroes of North Bay and surrounding area.

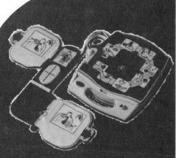

Time to put your experience to work.

For you!

If you are going to take the leap and try something new, consider a career where you run the show – where your ideas, your experience and your hard work pay off directly. If the idea of managing your own business has some appeal, we hope you'll take some time to find out more about becoming a Sun Life Financial advisor.

Kelly McQuoid, Associate Manager
Bus 705-472-8070 ext 228
kelly.mcquoid@sunlife.com
www.sunlife.ca

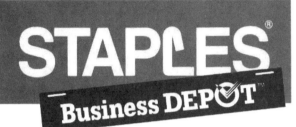

To: Our Teachers
Our Educational Assistants
Our Faculties
Our Guidance Counsellors
Our Administration Staff
Our Custodial Staff
Our Boards of Education

Thank You!

Merci beaucoup!

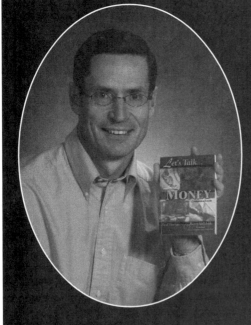

BDO Dunwoody LLP
Chartered Accountants
and Advisors

HONOURING THE HEROIC SPIRIT IN ALL OF OUR CITIZENS

142 Main Street West
North Bay, Ontario
P1B 2T5

(705) 495-2000

Callander Bay Dental Center

Congratulations Barry and Penny
on your project.

Congratulations to
Callander Bay Dental team and
supporters for raising $44,250.00 for
local children's charities in 2007.

299 Main St. N. Callander On. Tel: 705-752-1510

Salutes the many unsung heroes
who make North Bay a strong
and vibrant community.

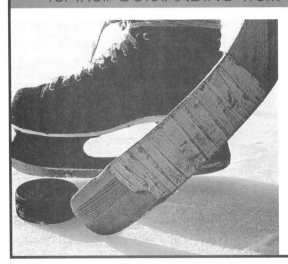

Community Futures Development Corporation
Société d'aide au développement des collectivités

195 First West/ouest, North Bay, ON, P1B 3B8
Tel/Phone: 705-476-8822   Fax/Télécopieur: 705-495-6038
www.neco.on.ca

NECO is a regional economic development organization, which invests in, and nurtures small business, and develops partnerships with private and public sectors to create and maintain jobs in our communities.

NECO est une organisation de développement économique régionale qui encourage et investit dans les petites enterprises, et développe des partenariats avec les secteurs publique et privé, dans le but de créer et maintenir des emplois dans nos collectivités.

Our Programs & Services

- Business Development Services
- Loans for Business Start-up and Expansion
- Community Economic Development Grants
- Young Entrepreneurship Program
- Mentorship Program
- Export Development Program

Nos programmes et services

- Services de développement des enterprises
- Investissement aux enterprises
- Programme de jeunes entrepreneur(e)s
- Initiative de planification d'entreprises
- Programme de mentorat
- Développement communautaire
- Programme de développement d'exportation

NECO… Develop Your Future with us!
NECO… Développez votre avenir avec nous!

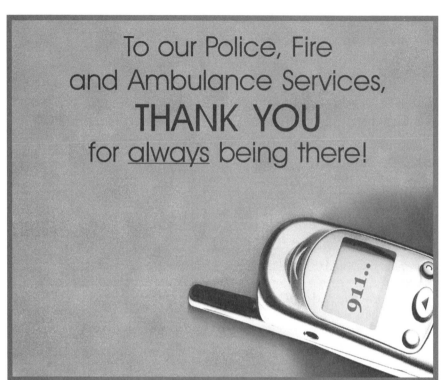
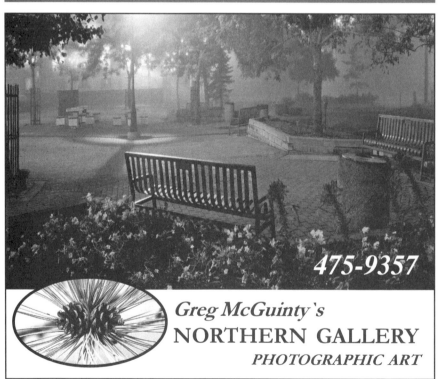

To all the local

I would like to personally acknowledge and congratulate all of the individuals who act as everyday heroes to people young and old throughout our community. It is your personal commitment and dedication that make a difference for people who look up to you. Your sacrifices go a long way to making this community a better place to live.

~ David Neil, President

PENNY TREMBLAY

Penny Tremblay, ACG, CL
President
Northern Lights Presentations
www.PennyTremblay.com
705-498-1818

❯ **Effective Communication**

❯ **Relationship Strategies**

❯ **Work / Life Balance**

❯ **Time Management**

❯ **Team Building**

❯ **Leadership Development**

❯ **Effective Presentation Building and Delivery**

If you are interested in writing to Penny Tremblay, receiving her free newsletter, *Leadership Tips*, or would like to inquire about speaking engagements, seminars or invite her to speak at an event, please direct all correspondence to:

Northern Lights Presentations

180 Sheriff Avenue, Suite 230
North Bay, Ontario Canada P1B 7K9
705-472-2528 ext. 202
info@northernlightspresentations.com
www.northernlightspresentations.com

The Right Decision Starts with Your People!

MEET YOUR CO-AUTHORS

PENNY TREMBLAY

Penny Tremblay has played a key role in the professional development of adults since 1989. She is the current President of Northern Lights Presentations, which offers Business Training & Corporate Communications services to assist organizations and individuals achieve their goals. While most of her efforts are focused locally in Northern Ontario, Penny is often invited to educate and motivate individuals at speaking engagements throughout Canada and the United States.

Northern Lights Presentations consults to organizations globally. Office and web solution consulting is a successful part of their business. The organization helps small to mid sized companies with creative marketing, brand development and website design strategies.

An effective communicator and leader, Penny has attained Advanced Communicator Gold status and Competent Leader designations with Toastmasters International and is currently working toward an elite designation of Accredited Speaker.

Penny's mission is to help millions of people achieve their goals. With a busy seminar schedule she addresses audiences on popular subjects of Communication, Leadership and Time Management and Work / Life Balance strategies. As an author, Penny writes monthly Leadership articles, which are published in several international journals, and circulated to recipients electronically upon request.

Recognizing the importance of leadership skills as the multiplier of success in one's career, Penny is passionate about introducing these skills to our youth in the secondary and post secondary education system.

Born and raised in Sudbury Ontario, Penny now resides in North Bay with her spouse David Neil, and enjoys family time with their three awesome kids, Kendra, Ryan and Sierra.

MEET YOUR CO-AUTHORS

BARRY SPILCHUK

Birthday: November 10, 1957 - Hamilton, ON
North Bay-ite: 1967-1978 and 1986 - present
Favorite Books: This one & Rings of Truth by Jim Britt
Favorite Movies: Mr. Smith Goes to Washington, It's a Wonderful Life
       The American President, When Harry Met Sally,
       Mr. Holland's Opus
Favorite TV Shows: West Wing, Mary Tyler Moore, Law & Order,
       M.A.S.H., Cheers, Studio 60, Seinfeld, Friends.

Favorite Teachers (just a few of many): Dr. Carruthers: Miss Nichols, Mrs. Smith & Roy Osburg; Centennial - Shirley Taylor W.J. Fricker: Rick Ferron; Chippewa High: Christine Cassidy, Bud McMartin, Eric Jarvi, Miss Hanson and Floyd MacMillan; Canadore College: Robin Smallwood, Dean McCubbin, Ken Cork, Rod Vincent, and Berny McGuaghey; From the School of Life: Mom, Dad, Tim, Karen, Jamie, Chrissy and Mike Spilchuk. God, Jesus Christ, Leland Val Vandewal, Jack Canfield, Mark Victor Hansen, Berny Dohrmann, Martin Rutte, Dr. Robert H. Schuller, Tim Piering, Lisa Nichols, Sharan Ro, Lydia Hale, Joel Roberts, Kristin Shepherd, David Stanley, Paul Barton, and people in general.

Pet Peeves: Unfairness, when someone takes advantage of someone else, bullies in school or business, rudeness.

Special Moments: Walking down the aisle November 15, 1980. The birth of our three "chimps." Our 25th anniversary. Every time I have apologized to one of our children. Being the first Canadian to coauthor a Chicken Soup for the Soul® book. Teaching for 11 years at a high-level business retreat in Los Angeles. Being, "unofficially," voted as one of Canada's Best Speakers. Being asked to walk in the Labour Day parade by the labour council when I was Chamber of Commerce President. Saying "YES" to this dream.

www.YMHbooks.com
1-705-497-5940
barry.s@ymhbooks.com

DIARY OF A DREAM
The You're My Hero™ Story

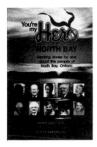

How does something like You're My Hero™ happen? We were working on another dream - raising $100 million for charity, doing a cross-country golf tour. We had a 38-foot motor home and were cruising through our ninth state in the USA when gas prices hit an all-time high. It was costing us over $400.00 a day to fill up the bus.

I kept praying for two things: 1) A major sponsor to underwrite our travel costs 2) Something we could leave behind as a legacy in every city we visited across the USA and Canada.

Three different times, I received the same answer to my first prayer: "You are supposed to be your own sponsor." I felt like Bill Cosby when he did the God and Noah's Ark comedy routine many years back. Each time, I got the same answer to my prayer, "You are supposed to be your own sponsor," I would curiously reply, "Say what? We do not have enough money to fill the bus with gas for 30 days and You want me to sponsor myself for a year?!?"

A short while later, an answer to my second prayer came in the form of grade six, twin girls in Flint, Michigan. They asked a friend of mine, "Can we do a Chicken Soup-like book for our classroom?"

This dream has gone through many phases and stages since the fall of 2005. What has evolved is this system - the You're My Hero™ System. The system that ensures everyone is involved - no one is left out - non-profit groups benefit and people take the opportunity to acknowledge their friends, their family and sometimes even themselves.

As of November 1, 2007, we have our second book in progress and have fielded inquiries from numerous cities across Canada and the United States about doing You're My Hero™ books for their cities.

The golf dream will continue, in a few years, with a sponsor - You're My Hero™ Books Ltd. God was right again. He always is.

Thank you to everyone who has caught and are catching the Hero-Bug. The grade six twins asked the perfect question. Thanks girls!

To quote another good book, "…and a child shall lead them."

Barry Spilchuk

Who Do You Know...

That would like to honour their heroes
And raise money for charity in the process?

**Here are just a few groups that can be served by:
YOU'RE MY HERO™ BOOKS**

You're My Hero™ - CITY Books
Celebrate your local heroes just like the people of North Bay, Ontario. They raised money for Nipissing Transition House, a women's shelter. Money was also raised for school projects.

You're My Hero™ - SCHOOL Books
Every child in every grade can go home and say, "Mom and Dad, I'm going to be in a book with a Chicken Soup guy!" Enhance literacy in a simple way - each child has to write only ONE story and put it on-line. You also raise money for school projects!

You're My Hero™ - CHURCH Books
The congregation is usually buying books in the Church bookstore, some of the books written by their Pastor. Why not let them WRITE the book about Heroes in your Church. You enhance the spirit of fellowship and raise a few dollars too!

You're My Hero™ - COMPANY Books
Acknowledging each other is the BEST way to grow your team and your company. For one flat fee let our team assemble a book about your team. It can enhance morale, teamwork and your bottom line!

**Visit our website: www.YMHbooks.com
Call: 1-705-497-5940 / Email: barry.s@ymhbooks.com**